Now All The Rage

Duncan Bush is the author of several prize-winning collections of poetry, and two novels, *The Genre of Silence* and *Glass Shot*. His collection of poems *Masks* was Welsh "Book of the Year" in 1995.

By the same author

Novels

The Genre of Silence
Glass Shot

Poetry

Aquarium
Salt
Masks
The Hook
Midway

Plays

Sailing to America

Now All The Rage

A NOVEL

Duncan Bush

Cf

Published by Colophon Books 2008

First published in Great Britain in 2008 by
Colophon Books
Godre Waun Oleu, Brecon Rd, Ynyswen, Penycae
Brecknockshire, SA9 1YY, UK

colofiction@live.com

ISBN 978-0-9559633-0-8

Set in Garamond

Printed and bound in Great Britain by
CPI Antony Rowe, Chippenham, Wiltshire

1

Never Dark

It was the car alarm going off just outside in the street which woke him. It didn't sound like his. He lay there startled, listening to its two-note modulation pitched between squeal and blare, squeal and blare, and again and again and again. Panic alarms, was that what they were called? That was what they sounded like. Especially at night, amplified by darkness. Panic and alarm. In regularised soundwaves. And in equal measure. Each volley of noise identical to the last, so that each new one was a diminishing shock but also, eventually, an increasing expectation.

He lay there listening to it.

Just as he thought he was going to start screaming in ululating unison, it stopped.

He lay there listening to it. The silence. For a moment the two-tone commotion seemed to continue, in some ghostly auditory after-image. Then there was calm. His wife's breathing still hadn't altered. But he was awake again. He was awake and already exhausted, the bleak exhaustion of the early hours. The longest hours before it's even light.

How early was it?

He groped for his wrist-watch on the bedside table. When he turned the face towards the window there was just enough of the drab orange light from the streetlamps to make out the hands. It was ten to five. Ten to five, and he was exhausted. Late to bed and early to wake. Makes a man healthy and wealthy and

Ache. Bake. Cake.

No.

Dake. Eake. Don't exist.

Fake.

Stealthy, unhealthy and fake.

He lay there listening intently to his wife's breathing, knowing that she too was awake, was only feigning sleep. But her breathing didn't alter. He was exhausted. But as always when he was conscious at this hour - and lately it seemed he was conscious at this hour more and more often - his mind was seething.

One of the finest minds of the century.

Perhaps the greatest mind of his generation.

Constantly engaged in the constant search for. Truth. Honour. Freedom. Justice between men. The reason why we're here.

FADE IN on APPLAUSE.

"Good evening, ladies and gentlemen. It gives me great pleasure to welcome you to tonight's special, commemorative edition of *Desert Island Discs*.

"Our castaway tonight will be familiar to some of you, especially those of you - friends and celebrities - who are in the invited audience here. But to those of you who are watching on television nationwide, he may be less well known.

"In fact, he's hardly what might be called a household name. Not yet. But that, of course, is part of the justification for a programme like this. In fact, when I agreed to host this programme, to take over from Sue Lawley, that was the one condition I insisted on. That from now on we'd spend less time in giving free publicity to the already and, it has to be said, often undeservedly famous, and start paying some attention to the unjustifiably ignored.

"And, as soon as that was decided, the first person I thought of to initiate this new programme was our guest tonight, Guy Hughes.

APPLAUSE

". . . Guy Anthony Hughes. One of the finest brains of the. Constantly engaged. The reason why we're here. . . "

APPLAUSE

Yes.

2

"A very good evening, ladies and gentlemen. *Bonsoir, mesdames et messieurs. Guten Nacht, meine Damen und Herren.* It gives me great pleasure to welcome you to this very special celebration coming to you live on tv, in front of a celebrity audience, here in

the BBC Television Centre

the Barbican

the Albert Hall.

"Tonight's events are to be broadcast simultaneously, on a number of channels, to our friends in Europe and the U.S.

"We're here tonight, ladies and gentlemen, to honour one of our most celebrated. . ."

Now his wife too was awake. Or rather, moving. As he'd suspected, she'd been awake all the time, timing her breathing to feign deep, uninterrupted sleep. Now she'd decided to come to consciousness slowly, as if out of hibernation. To move. She murmured something, pushing a hand against his side as if to thrust him gently from the bed.

"Car."

"*What?*"

"Your car. See if your car's alright."

He lay there, his mind seething at the interruption. She pressed her hand into his side again, more softly, as if to mitigate the request.

"Go on", she said indistinctly.

"It's a different alarm."

"Go and look."

"Do you think I don't know the sound of my own alarm?"

He lay there. He knew the sound of his own alarm. It was the whine in his head. Blood pressure, was it? Almost too high-pitched for human hearing. Except at night when you lay still and listened. Was it always there?

"Just go and see."

He knew he'd know no peace until he'd done what she said.

"For fuck's sake," he said savagely.

3

He threw the bedclothes back, swung his bare legs out of the bed and padded across to the lit curtains. Their bedroom window was never dark, even when the curtains were drawn.

He stood in the bay and stared down at the street. Cars were parked along both pavements, his own still angled between two others as tight to the kerb as the skill of long practice at backing into spaces not quite generous enough could achieve. He could even see the red light of its alarm system winking off and on in the nearside window.

"Is it alright?"

He said bitterly, "It's still fucking there."

He stayed at the window, gazing down into the street. There was no one, no movement.

"What's the matter?" his wife called.

"Nothing's the matter."

"Come back to bed. You're keeping me awake."

Her voice was irritable. And, just as, a minute earlier, he'd resented her pretending to be asleep, now he resented her alert wakefulness. Even when he woke up at five in the ack fucking emma he couldn't be alone.

There was already a dull grey light behind the roofs. He stared out. The Biblical phrase bowels of exhaustion came into his mind. That was how he felt. Exhausted, but faintly costive. Hollow but inwardly burdened. He stood looking at the houses opposite, regretting, as he did often, how the tone of the street had been lowered by various neighbours, mostly recent incomers, effecting what they thought of as improvements: style-less renovations done on the cheap. His was one of the few houses in the street which still had the brick frontage unstuccoed, the skewback arches still intact. And his was probably the only one with the original wooden sash-windows. Most of the other houses had replaced theirs with double glazing, with aluminium or white PVC frames. The one directly opposite now even had lozenged panes, glued-on strips meant to resemble leadwork. It was a house whose owners had left nothing to chance in the effort at prettification: it had Elizabethan windows, a Georgian front door, and the rucked curtains in the front windows were raised in the middle, like a lady's skirt over an instep, a coy style meant to resemble Victorian. Worst of all, the brickwork had been faced in contoured imitation-stone cladding, in random cream and pink. He never saw it, even in this dead orange light which universalised everything, without loathing for its owners, a pair of shell-suits with two children and a Toyota whose name he didn't even know. They didn't even have the sense to realise that original fabric was what appreciated, not make-overs done by jobbing cowboys from the back of a white van.

He despaired of it all sometimes. He despaired of it all all the time.

No: hated it. After the scientific conquest of scarcity and life's ceaseless filth came a teeming human crassness, fuelled by the pauperised imagination and the credit-card, and indomitable as the MRSA virus.

And they'd done it in full view of his front window.

He let the curtain fall back into its folds. His wife moved, and groaned. He stepped from the window-bay, which was largely occupied by the dressing table. It had three mirrors, pale upright rectangles: a broad one in the centre and a narrow one either side. Their proportions, and the angle at which the side-mirrors were set, corresponded to the big front window and raked side-panes in the embrasure of the bay itself. The mirrors stood at a slight backward tilt to show the face and shoulders of someone seated on the buttoned stool (which was now fitted into the narrow space left between the two sets of drawers for the sitter's legs). Not that anyone ever did sit there, so far as he knew. His wife usually put her makeup on in the bathroom, where the light was good and she could stand scrutinising herself in the mirror above the new half-octagonal washbasin, assuming (he had often thought with irritation) that searching, hard-eyed expression with which she tried to make herself more glamorous.

In fact, the dressing-table was almost never used as it was designed to be - by a seated woman with her makeup accoutrements in front of her and whatever else she needed in the shallow drawers to hand at either side. And its mirrors were, in this sense, of less importance than their plywood backs, which acted as screens, to reduce the sense that the windows of the houses opposite looked into the bedroom. However, by reflecting the back of the room and expanses of the ceiling, the mirrors did help to give the bedroom an illusion of greater volume, as recommended for small rooms in those magazines - *Home and Garden, Period Homes, Country Life* - his wife was always reading on some envious compulsion of dissatisfaction and a lifetime's longing for a tall cream townhouse or a country pile.

Sometimes, though, he himself used the mirrors. Stood in front of them to button a shirt, perhaps. Or just to look at himself.

He did so now, as he stood there in his underpants and vest.

Looked at himself. In the large central mirror first, though he was reflected in the side mirrors too, as in a triptych.

No, he thought. Triptychs were usually hung flat to the wall.

This angled arrangement was more like one of those hinged icon screens that could be stood with its wings set open, at a slight rake, facing outwards. Or they could be closed like doors on the central image of the godhead.

He drew his stomach muscles in tighter, pivoting to see the improvement, first in the big mirror then in the other two. It struck him that this movement resembled the preening motions of a body-builder showing off his development, as if for several cameras, that fixed grimace of teeth above it. Like the yellowed grin in a dead horse's skull. That was one of the drawbacks of being an artist, he thought: you saw yourself as objectively as a hanging side of meat.

And not just an artist:

But a sculptor of increasingly international renown

A photographer, magisterial exponent of the candid shot, snapper of unconsidered trifles. ("He is my master. His work has taught us all to see." - Henri Cartier-Bresson).

And, in recent years, a maker of some of the most

fascinating and provocative short films on video ever to have

"What are you doing?" his wife hissed.

She flounced over in the bed like a glove picked up and flung down anyhow.

"I've got to get up in a bloody hour!" she complained.

He went back to the bed and slipped into it on his side. His wife flounced over again, as if to ensure her back was to him. He lay there looking up at the ceiling, which to his eyes by now seemed almost lit from the curtains.

He listened to his wife's breathing. It slowed. Then it was almost inaudible, as if she'd stopped breathing.

He lay there.

"By the way, ladies and gentlemen, perhaps it's time to share a secret with you. This is the first time that Guy Hughes and I have ever met. Isn't that true, Guy?"

"That's absolutely true, Kirsty."

LAUGHTER.

"But of course it's also true that I've known *of* Guy Hughes by reputation - known your *work*, I mean - for many years, and it's one of those funny things, but I have to admit I've always sort of *felt* I knew you. I mean, I'd never even seen a photograph of you - because I know you shun the camera, you've always hated publicity and so on - but I already had a mental *image* of you. I'm babbling, aren't I?"

LAUGHTER

"No, it's true! I did! You know, the way you have an image of someone sometimes?"

"So do I measure up to it?"

LAUGHTER.

"No - I mean, yes!"

"You were expecting a taller man?"

LAUGHTER.

"I mean, you're very different. Shyer than I'd imagined. You're more reticent, let's say. But more *imposing*, somehow. Are a shy person?"

"No. Not really. I don't have time for shyness. But I've

always hated arrogance. Vanity. Self-importance."

"Yes, you see that in so many stars. But you've never sought the spotlight?"

"Never. I've always seen that as a weakness. As a form of inner doubt."

"But, as I say, many of us feel we've known you through your work for many years. You've been an icon for so many people in the arts. But it's only now you're all the rage that you're starting to get the sort of international reputation, the media attention -"

"Stop twitching!" his wife hissed furiously. "I'm going to start sleeping in the other room if you keep jerking about like that!"

He lay there, his mind shocked at the sudden interruption. One of the finest minds of. An icon to so many. The sort of media attention he was starting to.

He lay there. He had the idea for the triptych. A triple self-portrait. Himself as if reflected at slightly different angles in three mirrors. He lay there thinking about it. Visualising it.

Or what if he used the dressing-table itself? (With the three self-portraits replacing the mirrors?)

An icon screen.

The whole concept incorporated into an installation, adapted out of a cheap white dressing-table bought from MFI or B & Q. And in MDF. Medium density fibreboard, with a sagging back and plastic knobs. Furniture for the modern boudoir. Which of them had chosen it? And why? He supposed it was the kind of cheap furniture they'd bought when they first got married. The kind you could break up in your hands if you ever chose to, if your rage at the modern age and the built-in decrepitude of its artefacts ever took you that far. In fact the fucking thing was already falling apart, not so much from actual use or wear as from the weight of its own flimsy components. The runners to two of the drawers had dropped, so that instead of sliding in and out each drawer collapsed on the one underneath when you tried to open or close it. And the side uprights moved if you pushed them, the rectangular boxes which framed the drawers swaying into parallelograms.

It was the perfect cultural symbol for post-Millennium Britain.

But for an artwork that would last, he wanted something more substantial. Not antique, nothing pretentious. Just plain, strong, simple. Something from the Thirties or Forties. Or wartime Utility ware, okay, it was only oak veneer but underneath it was well-made and solidly-built in pine or deal, with a back of three-ply board and tenoned drawers on fitted wooden rails. You used to be able to pick up stuff like that in junk-shops for a few quid. Now, of course, it was probably fashionable again. People had had enough of self-collapsible furniture, built to last only as long as most marriages did these days. Or only as long as the couple's residence on some raw jerry-built honeymoon estate of "first-time buyers", before the act of moving it to a new address - a bigger mortgage, or one of the couple moving out when the marriage broke up - shook it apart in the removal van.

No, solidity was coming back, he felt. And he had an instinct for these things: for style, taste. He'd have to flick through *Traditional Homes* or *Period Living,* old issues of which were scattered all over the house, in collapsed piles under the sofa or slippery and dangerous underfoot as patches of ice on the living-room or bedroom carpet. He rarely opened them except when seated on the lavatory. But his wife always made sure there were several in the bathroom, perhaps to invite ruminative attention to the renovations they'd had done there, based on bathrooms she'd seen in just such magazines: the octagonal mirror, the semi-octagonal washbasin and matching bath, and the black-and-white floor-tiles. Of course, the tiling was all wrong. The man who'd laid the tiles had said they should be laid on the diagonal, lozenge-style. It was a small room, the man had pointed out, and diagonal rows increased the sense of floor-space. Also, the walls weren't perfectly square. Laid on the right-angle, the tiles would work out to an irregular cut strip at the end of each row.

But his wife had told him to lay it that way anyway: chessboard-style.

"I think it looks more stylish," she'd said. "For a bathroom"

- meaning that was how it had been in the full-page colour photo of the full-size colour bathroom she'd seen in the magazine.

What she didn't even seem to realise, he meditated with a curious futile rancour, was that a really elegant bathroom had to be just that, anyway: a room for taking a bath in. You shouldn't have to perform all your other bodily necessities there as well. The "suite" of matching bath, washbasin and toilet was already, on the grounds of style, space and sanitation, a compromise, another triumph for the petty bourgeois dream that no addition of a matching bidet could disguise. Especially in peach or apricot or avocado, that fruitererer's colour range now irredeemably dated.

Even sharing a bathroom with another person was a compromise, he decided. In fact a fucking affront. Everyone should have their own all-in-one *chambre de toilette,* and on an appropriate scale, like ones you saw in National Trust properties. The one at Castle Drogo, say, which they'd visited last year in that week they'd spent in Devon, the last castle built in England, designed by Edwin Lutyens for the Drew grocery dynasty. A baronial-size bathroom with a huge bath and rows of copper jugs to fill it with, with an easy-chair to read the newspaper in and a coffee-table, there'd even been a little burn-mark showing where the paterfamilias's morning cigar had once rolled from its ashtray. And the walls panelled in mahogany, with a bank of steps up to an arrow-slit window and a view. Of your own spread-out woods and fields, and a county or two beyond them. Yes. That was where Old Man Drew withdrew. When he wanted peace and a soak. Or a smoke. Or a stroke. Drew of the Home and Colonial.

Along with Scott of the Antarctic
Carleton-Browne of the F.O.
and Barlasch of the Guard.

His eyes were closing. His mind was wavering, burning out.

But he turned his head and looked again at the dressing table in the window-space. From this angle its triple mirrors reflected only inclined planes of ceiling half-lit in the city's ubiquitous, inescapable orange glow. He envisaged himself in the

10

frames, depicted as in a Bacon triptych, a hanging side of pork, the painting done very directly onto board sized with gesso and set in the little metal half-moons which clasped the cheap arched mirrors in place, the three self-portraits hinged like an icon screen, symmetrical inward-facing images of him, in singlet and underpants, unshaven but imposing, a mind to so many, one of the finest of his century, one of the dives on Thirty Second Street, one of the low, dishonest decades, one of these days.

2

His Best Day

The alarm going off just after seven woke him. He lay there without moving, though his brain jarred to its ring – or rather, shrill. It had a peculiarly insistent, unsettling battery-powered two-note shrill. Finally, his wife too could bear it no longer. It was on her side of the bed. She groaned and groped for the clock, fumbled with it one-handed and switched it off. She lay back again hopelessly, as if to gather strength. Then with another groan she threw back the bedcovers and forced herself up out of the bed and into a standing position. She shuffled across the room to the door; then he heard her in the bathroom. Water into water, then water flushing. He lay feeling the coolness from her side of the bed. Usually she closed the triangle of turned-back bedclothes after getting up. But this morning she'd deliberately left the bed half-open to express her annoyance at lost sleep, at being woken again in the night by his restlessness and insomnia.

He lay there, waiting for his wife to leave the bathroom so he could get up. They couldn't bear crossing first thing in the morning. But then he pushed the bed-clothes back over on his wife's side and burrowed deeper, luxuriously. He'd just remembered it was Thursday, and on Thursdays he didn't have to be in college until eleven. And that last night he'd thought to set the radio alarm, on his side of the bed, for an hour later - for just after eight.

*

He was awakened by the voice of the Foreign Secretary. He lay there listening to it, then to the voice of John Humphrys, who was conducting the interview.

It was gone eight. His wife must have left.

He lay listening to the Foreign Secretary.

John Humprys gently repeated his question. The Foreign Secretary made the same answer in not quite identical words.

By now Guy was fully awake, but still exhausted. He lay there listening with a sort of futile incredulity at the patient, pedantic evasions.

Of all the detestable politicians in the current Government, he decided, he detested this one most. The phrase *weasel words* might have been coined expressly for that slightly prim, rodent-like mouth, those alert ratlike eyes that were too small even behind the enlarging lenses of the metal-rimmed spectacles which advertised myopia without conferring intellectuality.

He and Guy were almost the same age, and Guy had detested him for many years now – in fact ever since he'd begun his remorseless and unstoppable clamber to public notice as leader of the National Union of Students, when Guy himself had also been a student activist. He'd naturally started disliking him on a more personal count now that, after years in Opposition, he'd eventually come into Government - and to positions of real prominence and influence – so that he, Guy, was confronted with him on the futile, recurrent, daily basis that listening to successful politicians on current affairs programmes on the radio ensured.

But a little while ago this dislike had increased to an outraged and vindictive hatred after Guy had happened to read in a newspaper how the other man had bought a weekend cottage in Oxfordshire - whereupon, seeing that he was Home Secretary at that time, the Ministry of Defence had bought the adjoining cottage too, which was to be kept permanently empty "for security reasons".

No crass or troublesome neighbours for him in his new, and doubtless delightful surroundings in the Cotswolds. No one overlooking his garden, looking into his windows. No car alarms in his street. No underclass yobs leaving rubbish in his front porch. No one to disturb his rural peace. Not at Jack Straw's Castle.

You didn't understand the privileges of power, the sheer opulence of it, until you read a news item like that. You couldn't even keep track of it: the opportunities and backhanders, the sweeteners and the perks, the endless bloody perks, eagerly offered, airily presumed: all these were taken for granted, the newspapers never even mentioned them - the sumptuous expenses and the ministerial cars and the drivers and the secretaries and the endless free lunches, the never having to put your own hand into your trouser pocket for anything except to scratch your balls.

And now this shrewd and sedulous second-rater had moved from Home Secretary to Foreign Secretary. A post which came with a grace-and-favour country residence as well, a little palace in the orbital shires, rent-free and fully staffed.

Guy flung the bedclothes back and swung his bare feet out onto the floor. There was no rest from the wicked. Even in bed. Even here he was harassed. Even on a Thursday morning.

And what about that other one, Meacher, another prim-mouthed New Labour puritan whose teeth looked as if they gave him trouble, another M.P. from a safe working-class seat of post-industrial malaise whose constituents no doubt saw less and less of him as his star rose. This was the environmentalist, the rambler's friend: the one who'd spoken out about the problems caused by second-home owners in areas like the Cotswolds, and then it turned out he'd recently paid a cool half-million for a bijou cottage there as well. It turned out in fact, according to the newspaper, that he owned nine homes in all. Nine homes. A man with a faintly suffering look, yet whose air of moral piety was one that only the true hypocrite would never need to manufacture.

Socialists? It was enough to make you bleed at the ears.

As he sat on the lavatory in the tiny bathroom, in their

small semi-detached house in its run-down suburb, Guy picked up a copy of *Country Life* and opened it. It was a new issue, this month's. He stared at the property advertisements with almost incredulous envy. Knightsbridge Regency cream stucco. Manor houses. Castles in their grounds. Vast lawns mown green and silver towards parkland trees. Price upon application. Premiership footballers only. Or oil sheikhs from the brutal kingdoms.

It hurt the heart even to see such things. He tossed the stiff glossy magazine to the floor, and sat there in his stench. He could still hear the bedside radio, voices in the other room, the endless talk, talk, talk of modern life.

It was only when he flushed the lavatory and stepped under the hissing showerhead that it was drowned out.

"Good morning, ladies and gentlemen. This is John Humprys. This morning we introduce something new on the *Today* programme. It's called 'Meet The Public', and it'll be a regular spot in the programme where you, members of the listening public - taxpayers, voters, citizens - get the opportunity to interrogate a politician of your choice. This idea is the brainchild of the artist Guy Hughes, who is also one of our most excoriating political commentators. And, very fittingly, it's he who has been chosen to launch the whole thing today by conducting our first interview in this new format. The politician he's chosen to question today is Michael Meacher, M.P."

"Good morning, Mr Meacher. I'd like to start off by looking at your property interests, if we may."

"Good morning, Mr Hughes. Er, property interests?"

"Yes. You do own various properties, I believe? Numerous properties, one might even say."

"I was, um, under the impression that we'd be discussing politics."

"I don't know what gave you that impression. I certainly gave no assurances as to how the interview -"

No.

No. Already he'd let the bastard put him on the back foot.

And he was being too wordy. Pompous-sounding. It was being on radio. He'd let a radio voice take over his own. He had to adapt quicker than that. Meeting them on the BBC was playing them on their own turf, or as good as.

"Property interests?"

SILENCE.

"You do own a substantial number of properties, don't you?"

"I was actually under the impression that we'd be discussing Government policy."

SILENCE.

Guy Hughes held it. Just long enough for it to register.

As silence.

His.

"It was made clear to you that this interview would be wide ranging, wasn't it?"

"I'm here as a representative of the Government, and I'm happy to discuss Government policy on the environment."

The light, complacent tone of one deft at turning an interview.

SILENCE

"Or, indeed, as an Member of Parliament, the concerns of my constituents."

SILENCE.

Again Guy held it. Just long enough.

Long enough for it to start to hiss.

"I'm interested in the fact that your constituents mostly live in crummy terraced streets, while you buy a rumoured ninth home in the Golden Ellipse. So perhaps you could just answer the question instead. It was made clear to you that this interview would be wide ranging, wasn't it?"

"I don't think your listeners are interested in my private affairs."

SILENCE.

For a third time Guy let the hiatus lengthen, not responding to the Minister's lightly mocking tone. Instead he let it echo in its own void.

Already John Humphrys was leaning forward intently, but the producer was half-crouched at the banked switches of his console, peering anxiously in through the glass. Soon he'd be making the cutthroat signal with his forefinger. Silence, the prolongation of silence, was the one thing that terrified these radio pros. They thought of radio as an empty room they had to fill with voices, voices talking, singing, babbling, always voices. Silence unnerved them.

What they didn't understand was that by now the Minister was unnerved too. And that all over the country people were leaning forward to their radio set, turning it up. In kitchens, at breakfast tables, in traffic out on the M25. They'd all sensed that with this new format – and, above all, this new interviewer - the tired format designed for the free promulgation of the usual programmatic message, the daily and hourly party political broadcast from Westminster to the suckers, had altered forever. They'd sensed a new intensification of the medium of radio itself, a new, steelier style of political interrogation, silence as a forensic tool. It was out of the faint hiss and crackle of that interference you heard as if for the first time that the lie was spelt out.

It was the hiss and crackle of historic truth.

"Wasn't it? Yes or no?"

"Yes. But I don't think . . ."

Was that the phone?

He switched the shower off. The phone was ringing downstairs in the hall. He stepped out of the shower cubicle and stood there, listening to it. It rang and rang and rang again with that dispassionate regularity a phone has when you have to leave the shower and are rapidly trying to dry yourself in time to answer it, its ringing underlining your own furious haste by displaying neither urgency nor lack of it.

It stopped ringing just as he left the bathroom with the towel round his waist, legs still streaming

"*Fuck* it," he screamed in furious incredulity. "Fucking *bastard* phone!"

He completed his outraged journey down the stairs to the hall table anyway. He picked up the receiver and punched 1471 with the point of his forefinger.

A recorded feminine voice with mechanical inflections informed him that the caller had withheld the number.

"*Fuck you too, cunt,*" he shouted at the phone.

He held it in his hand and stared at it.

There was, of course, a calculated way of "withholding" your number. If you were a BT subscriber you merely dialled 141 - was it? – prior to the number you were trying to reach. But the robot voice uttered the same formula of words if the call was made from a mobile phone, whatever the network provider. So in practice you never knew, with an unanswered call, if the caller was intentionally trying to conceal their own number or not. In this instance the call might simply have been from his wife, ringing him on her mobile on her way to work, to remind him of something or other. On the other hand, it could have been from anybody else. It could even have been someone trying to call her. Someone not knowing if she'd left yet, or if her husband was still there. Someone who didn't want the number traced. . . (The kind of thought, he thought, from which no husband could be free.)

He took the handset up into the bathroom. Just in case. Just in case the fucking caller, his wife or whoever the fuck it was, rang again when he was getting himself properly dry or dressing. And made him hurry down the fucking stairs again.

The phone was still there on the glass shelf above the semi-octagonal washbasin when he got back at 4.30, and found he had to look for it so he could ring his wife to find out what time she'd be home. Thursday was his best day. He started late and finished early.

Which makes a man healthy and wealthy and burly.A n d Thursday, 2 to 3.30 was Life Drawing.

Or Still Life ("In The Old Girl Yet"') as a colleague of his,

Ron Spicer, had described it (wittily, Guy thought, given the old girl in question).

The life model was a woman in her sixties whom he'd inherited when he took over the Life Drawing class, and who, it seemed, had been modelling at the art school for nearly twenty years. Her name was Emmie. Her age could not be held against her, of course, at least in principle. The primary requirements of a life model were not beauty or youth or proportion but stillness, the ability to maintain a pose. Nevertheless, whatever Emmie had looked like in her forties, when she'd started modelling, the *Maja Desnuda* she was not, not now, and the sight of her belly drooping like a slack belt-bag, the empty pouches of her breasts, the varicose veins in her thighs and the greying bush made Guy think more of pathologists' slabs than artists' couches.

Nature morte, as the French term had it.

But then, there had always been something clinical about Life Drawing, something which sent through the male member a cold shiver of horror rather than a warm flush of tumescence. Though that of course was the point of it. Life Drawing was about training students to see what was there to draw and to draw only what they could see. Non-kinetic art. The smooth lines of photographic models, the sleekness of an Elle MacPherson or a Naomi Campbell, merged into the silky backside of the neo-Platonic Ideal, which was the stereotype, by definition easier to draw.

In any case, he thought, feet, hands, breasts, knees, nipples were not erotic in themselves, and were rarely eroticised by nakedness. What conferred eroticism was the bangle, hinting at slavery. The cunningly positioned fold, concealing while inviting entry. Clothing, paradoxically, was what eroticised. What adorned what D.H. Lawrence termed the bursten fig.

He thought again of the white-stitched hem of the tee-shirt against Claire Tucker's sun-browned neck. Her long hair had been pinned up, so he could see the microscopically-tiny gold hairs that swarmed to the light at her tendoned nape. The brown mole in the hollow of her strongly pronounced clavicle. The grain of her pores. He could smell the wisteria scent she used.

Had he spent too long standing at her easel again? A class noticed things like that. Him taking so much notice of her.

He switched on MTV with the tv handset and stood looking at the screen. It was the cartoon filler, which you often seemed to catch by chance when you switched on, and so not by chance at all: a 20-second clip of animation advertising the channel itself and which, slotted in between music videos, over the day, a twenty-four-hour day of non-stop broadcasting, probably amounted to an hour or more of time when music copyright fees didn't have to be paid. It was a one-off expenditure, and a small one, and with no repeat fees. He knew how the system worked. He was almost a part of it. They just found a couple of talented young animators straight out of art college and sold them the chance of making a short advertising clip and having their work seen all over the world a couple of hundred times a day, and paid them a measly couple of hundred quid for doing so, in that way saving thousands.

This particular one was a good piece of animation. It showed a male figure in silhouette, first spinning on the floor in a break dance, then springing to his feet and strutting in a Michael Jackson moonwalk. Guy stood there watching it, admiring the movement. Knowledge of these things had come some way since Muybridge. But, like everyone else, Guy had seen the clip so often now that it had finally become what it was always intended to be, a delaying tactic, a way of engendering impatience or frustration.

He went into the kitchen and cleared the table of the breakfast things he'd left there that morning.

When he went back into the living room, there was a music video on, one he'd seen before, one everyone had seen before. It was Britney Spears again. The one he was always waiting for was the new one by Destiny's Child.

He sat down on the sofa and watched anyway.

Britney Spears strutted and pouted at the head of a team of dancers in that way she had, all puppyfat and pink lip-gloss. Her eyes had their usual intent and calculating vacancy. At this moment a million adolescent males, all over the world - in Sweden, Israel and the USA, in Malta, Yalta and Gibraltar - wanted nothing more than to masturbate over her chubby brown belly and rub it in like Johnson's Baby Oil, and she gave the impression that she knew of this and found it good.

He looked at his watch. It was 4.55. The house had that incriminating afternoon silence he loved: the silence not only of emptiness but of complicity. His wife probably wouldn't be home for another hour. But, given flexitime working, it was always safer to phone her and check.

Which was when he discovered the phone wasn't on its holder.

He looked in all the appropriate places: on the table, on the floor beside the sofa, in the small kitchen. Then he looked in all the appropriate places again, more carefully, lifting newspapers, books, home-style magazines.

He even looked in the fridge in case he'd put it in there with the butter after breakfast.

It was incomprehensible. How could you lose a telephone?

Who'd used it last?

He looked in all the downstairs rooms.

It wasn't on the stairs either.

Eventually Guy went up the stairs into the bedroom, and then into the bathroom, if only out of a kind of vexed incredulity and in that Kafkaesque way of the petitioner at the Gates of the Law who comes there only to give himself the respite of knowing that he has left no stone unturned, an act which gives only an illusion of respite or of the prospect of respite since another failure can only be succeeded by another journey, though this too equally pointless in its turn.

But as soon as he walked into the bathroom he saw the handset on the glass shelf above the washbasin, and recalled how he himself had come to leave it there.

He punched in the digits with his forefinger. Then, when the girl with the estuarine whine she thought of as a genteel public-speaking voice answered, asked for his wife's extension.

The extension number rang and rang. He stood there listening to it. It went on ringing in that dispassionate way with which a phone rings, displaying neither urgency nor lack of it, while you come to the gradual sense that there is no one at the other end to answer it.

Then, surprising him, the receiver was lifted and a male voice answered.

"Yes?"

The single, curt word, as if the speaker had been interrupted in something both engrossing and of vital importance, an interruption close to a personal affront.

Guy asked for Mrs Hughes.

"Angela?" the man enquired in a note of somehow insolent surprise, as if the use of her married name and title were a novelty. "I'm afraid she's not here."

"Isn't that her office?"

"It's her phone too. But the point is, she's not in it," the man said. "The office, that is. Not just now."

"Her coat's here," he added after a moment. "I *think* that's her coat. She must be somewhere around. Why not try later?"

"Can I leave a message?" Guy said, sensing the man was about to put the phone down, and more from an instinctive desire to obstruct that impatient wish than for any specific reason.

"If you'll just let me find something to write with."

There was exasperation in the man's voice, that of one whose good nature was now being put upon beyond measure, and for the twentieth time that day.

There was a delay, an audible search of a desktop, a drawer opened and slammed shut, then a second drawer, a mutter of almost incredulous vexation.

"Now I need something to write on," the man said finally.

Guy stood there waiting, listening. Silence. A scuffle of papers, a sheet torn from its block. All these movements had the pointedness, the almost pictorial clarity of radio sound-effects.

"Okay," the man said finally. "Shoot."

Guy already felt like doing so. One to the palate out of a muzzle that had had already smashed its way in through the teeth. One of those fine sprays of blood on the ceiling. A slow sit down against a smeared wall.

Instead Guy asked the man to leave the message that Guy had called.

And, as soon as he said so, wished he hadn't. As soon as he'd been told his wife was out of the office, he should have merely asked when she was expected back and rung off. After all, he'd only needed to assure himself that she was still in work. That she had not already left early for the day, as she did sometimes on a Thursday because she had her Keep Fit class that evening. That her coat was there.

"Guy," repeated the other man in a way that may have been sardonic. "Are you the husband?"

"That's right," Guy said, a little defensively. People did sometimes repeat his name in a dry or amused tone. But had the other man really said "the husband"? What did *the* husband mean? (Instead of *her* husband?)

"And who am I speaking to?" Guy asked.

"Oh, I just work here," said the man. Then, quickly, added: "Okay. Thanks, Guy." And put the phone down.

Guy put his down too.

He stood there, staring at it.

But then he was distracted from it by his own priorities. The house was silent. He stood there listening to it. But it was no longer a silence of invitation and complicity. It was now one which he'd unthinkingly, stupidly threatened with interruption in the form of the anticipated return call from his wife. And so, until she *did* call, and they'd had the usual otiose conversation about when exactly she was likely to be home, he'd be on edge. In expectation of the phone ringing. In impatience to have that conversation done and over with. Until then he had no option but to waste part of this rare, this luxurious, this criminal solitude in waiting to have its length fixed and confirmed.

23

3

Finishing Early

Or he could take it off the hook. As the saying was.

A phrase out of the days of wall-phones, when there was an actual hook to take it off. The days when you could leave a phone hanging, swinging on its cord, the way it does in old films after a bullet into the booth shortens conversation and everything else, the fink sliding down the wall, leaving the smear on the paintwork, the voice at the other end still saying, "Hello . . . Lou? Lou?".

The days when, if you didn't want to be interrupted by an incoming call, you just lifted the phone off the receiver and anyone trying to reach you got the Engaged Tone and knew they would have to try again later.

But, with this type of cordless modern electronic phone, taking the handset from its console or cradle (or whatever the fuck they called it in the instruction booklet) didn't deactivate it. You could take it into the garden and still get calls on it. The only way you could stop calls was by changing it from receiver to transmitter mode. Which you did by pressing the *Call* button to get the Dialling Tone. Then you could put the phone down somewhere.

But the problem then was this: it was an extremely *insistent* Dialling Tone. So much fucking so that if you laid the phone down in the same room - as he now found, once he'd done so and was seated again – it was audible from several feet away: a faint unbroken whine, between a mosquito and a wasp.

Or the note of a flatlining screen in the cardiac ward.

He got up again and took the handset out into the hall.

But then, as he was doing so, the continuous note of the Dialling Tone modulated automatically, on the completion of a certain period of time, into a rapid, broken succession at the same pitch: the Engaged Tone anyone calling that number now would hear.

This rapid note was even more audible, more urgent, more unsettling.

He listened to it. He stood there, phone in hand, staring with dislike and irritation at this lightweight, ergonomic plastic object in two-tone greys which was the modern telephone; and he thought with nostalgia of the classic old-fashioned heavy black bakelite phone with a shiny chromium-plated dial and a fabric-covered cord, like the one in *Dial M For Murder* - which he'd shown the First Year students only the other week, part of his Hitchcock programme. In those days, to stop incoming calls you simply lifted the handpiece out of the little sprung rests of the receiver, and laid it on its side on the telephone table. Hooked, hooded for discretion at the mouthpiece, it burred away quietly to itself at the end of its cord, incommunicado while the crime was perpetrated or furthered in an elegant service flat.

But in those days the London phone book had been just that: a single close-printed volume in an unvandalised kiosk: a red, many-paned kiosk, the design classic of George Gilbert Scott: and you had a home number (four digits, typed on a ribbon typewriter on the white cardboard disc inserted at the middle of the dial) and your own local exchange: Fremantle, Sloane, Welbeck. Mayfair, Maida Vale.. . How evocative, those names. The London of *Hue and Cry* and *Passport to Pimlico*.

Now they wouldn't allow you just to lay a phone on one side and forget about it. Technology couldn't stand being ignored. It was always in your face. That was what it did. Got in your face. So instead you had this fucking thing made like a cheap toy beeping at you, just loud enough to be comfortably within the range of normal hearing. A Panasonic pacemaker.

He laid the handset on the stairs, went up for what he wanted, then came back into the living room and closed the door. He'd just re-seated himself when her saw the cat was in the room with him. It sat there too, staring at him in the baleful, accusing way cats have. It was his wife who called herself a cat person. He wasn't, much. He got up, opened the door, and ushered the cat out with his foot, pushing it with the point of his shoe. As he closed the door again, the handset was still beeping on the stairs.

He suddenly realised where he'd already heard that persistent rhythm of dissonance and dislocation, pitched at that jabbing urgency: the car alarm which had woken him at five that morning.

Voluptuous Vikki, her head twisted, looked back at him over one shoulder. She was laughing. Her long blonde highlighted hair had been tucked behind her right ear so you could see her laughing face, her eager, expectant expression. It was one of those expressions women only ever wore in certain photographs. It was to show they were eager for, expectant of, a certain thing.   Legs astride, she stood on tiptoe against the fretted back of the white cast-iron garden chair. This stance served to accentuate the line and firmness of her legs, define the big muscle behind each thigh, tighten the globe of each buttock. Her buttocks were paler than the rest of her body.

Her hands were in front of her, holding the arched back of the chair as if for balance. Actually it was to emphasise her narrow waist and the slender muscles in her brown side. There was a band of darker tan across the small of her back, where the furrow of her spine was more pronounced. All the way up her back you could see the soft arrowheads of her vertebrae.

Christ she was lovely, Guy thought. Really lovely. Not like some of them. What you wouldn't like to do with a woman like that.

In the one picture she was wearing only the green-and-white hooped socks pulled up to mid-thigh.

She had a highly paid job in the City. But she was a weekend raver.

26

What were the excuses that made Vikki give in?

"When he closed the door of the Board Room and kissed me for the first time I thought, Mmm, you're an early riser. I'm not with that firm now. But I thought it wasn't such a bad way to keep your job. He put my hand down there and I undid his zip and put my hand in. It just sort of grew in it, like Topsy. I could see its outline bulging out of his Armani suit so I "

On tiptoe or not, there was a dimpling under the gluteus maximus. Gluten of cellulite. And at the top of the inner thigh, there where the shadow merged into the cleft, a depilated or shaven look. Sharkskin touch like an armpit, just where skin should be softest, merge into the silky backside of the neo-pornographic ideal.

In the best of the others she lay on her back in dry sand. Her lips parted. Her eyes closed as if against bright sun or in bliss. She wore a blue singlet like an athletics vest pulled up till it was no more than a tight, rucked band above her breasts. (Like, it struck him, the vest-like garment worn by Michelangelo's obviously homoerotic sculpture *The Slave*.) Her left hand was placed on her left breast, finger and thumb encircling the nipple as if to make the A.O.K. signal. The unsqueezed nipple was erect, its areola granular with papillae. But the skin of her upper arm was also gooseflesh, as if in a cool breeze from the unseen sea. Cooled him, too, his ardour. His harder and harder. And there, a flaw again, in the erected skin the grain and pore of things not airbrushed out, defined by a rim of shadow like a tiny dry sea on the moon: the circle of a girlhood vaccination mark.

"Or like when I had a job in Paris for two years - which is how I come to speak fluent French, by the way. It's not that I'm a snob but merchant bankers tend to be rich, and it doesn't hurt if they're good looking too. Also Jean-Pierre had a Bentley, a big aubergine-coloured one. I always think Rollses are ever so slightly vulgar. But Bentleys have real style. And it had dark tinted windows so we could go down into the executive car-park in the basement and screw in it, on the back seat. And he used to like to drive me around in it and have me pleasure him, as he used to call it. All this in rush-hour traffic! Once or twice we"

He looked down between the lifted knees, the blur of the Celtic F.C socks. There was the paler, less-sunned triangle. Defining the shock of the dark bush. The bursten fig.

"We'd even pull up alongside police cars, and he'd let his window down and sit there looking at the red light, and me with my head in his lap! And I found it incredibly arousing to be doing that, in daylight, in the middle of a city! Other times we'd drive at night "

Her right hand reached under her, splayed wide. To her stretched frilly panties, ever so slightly vulgar. The parted lips. For anyone to see. Her head was twisted to look up as she did it. To watch you as *you* did it.

"Through the Bois de Boulogne, where all the working girls were - the professionals. And he liked me to do it to him then too. He was married, of course - with a really beautiful wife. All the best men are! But we had a wonderful affair for that month or so when I was working for his company, just driving around in his Bentley. As they say, Paris is the most romantic city in the world! And I found it incredibly exciting to come again and again on his white leather seats, because whenever I met Jean-Pierre he liked me to leave my knickers off. Now I know why men find leather so exciting!"

His eyes were closed as if against bright sun or in bliss.

Fais-moi ça, she whispered.

Fais-moi ça, mon gorille. With your big aubergine-coloured one.

Now, now, she was pleading.

Sur ton cuir. Sur ton beau cuir fleur de peau.

"What are you doing?"

His wife stood in the open doorway open-mouthed. She gripped the handset of the phone.

They stared at each other in startled terror, as if each confronting a stranger in the house.

28

He lay in the armchair, legs sprawled out in front of him, trousers hobbling his ankles. He was holding the magazine up in one hand. He quickly put it over what he was had in the other.

"What does it look like I'm fucking doing?" he managed to scream.

Instinctively, it was accusatory. His only hope of mitigation lay in trying to make the offence hers.

And indeed his wife's gaze faltered, as if accepting dreadful wrong.

Then she turned and left the doorway.

He laid down the magazine quickly, stood. Bent, pulled up his trousers. Stuffed himself in, put himself away, the turkey's wattled head under its wing. Adjusted his dress before leaving.
The magazine lay on the seat face down, splayed wide on its stapled fold. For anyone to see. He snatched it up, closed its double-spread, Voluptuous Vikki still spread out. But now he didn't know what to do with it, except not to go out with it in his hand, like his grandfather walking back up the garden from the outside shithouse, the *Daily Herald* tucked under one arm.

He righted the chair-cushion, which had slid down under his sprawled body; then slipped the magazine underneath it, face down. Later he' could smuggle it back upstairs to its place in his green metal filing cabinet, among his do-it-yourself mags.

But now he had to he go out into the hall. What she thought of him doing *this* himself didn't bear contemplating But he went on into the kitchen.

His wife was standing there. She seemed to be waiting for him, and in some impatience; but when he came in she turned her back and went quickly to the electric kettle. She took it and filled it at the tap. She set it on its stand and clicked the switch. The red light came on and the kettle made that sound as the element started to heat the water.

"I'm making tea," she said in desperate pointlessness.

He watched her for a moment.

"That'll teach you to come in without knocking," he said with the bluff, unembarrassable heartlessness that had become the only posture open to him.

But his eyes, on his wife's, felt like a sick dog's.

In any event, her eyes slid away from his. Her embarrassment seemed real, distressed, beyond dissemblance.

She had her back to him and was staring out of the window at the wall of the house next door. That's what people do in moments of great trauma, he realised. They stand and stare at nothing. Not moving. Only points of anxiety stirring in that pursed fixity of gaze. He noticed that she still had her coat on. The phone lay on its back on the kitchen table, where she'd brought it in from the living room doorway. She must have seen it lying on the stairs as soon as she let herself in through the front door. Or she'd heard the insistent broken note it was emitting. Now, switched off, it lay there silent, a small dead armadillo.

He tried repeating his tone of defiance: "What are you doing home at this fucking time anyway?"

"I finished early," she said miserably.

They stood not quite facing, but their stances somehow confrontational. He saw that her chest was heaving, and realised his was too. Again he noticed that she still had her coat on. So whose coat had been left hanging on the peg in her office?

"I rang the office," he said. "Somebody said you were still there."

He said this accusingly, as if he'd only been caught out as the result of a deception or deliberate falsehood for which she was to blame.

"Well, I wasn't," she said, goaded to a defiance of her own. "So you didn't have as much bloody time as you thought, did you?"

This was such a merciless statement of the obvious that it shocked them both. She started to take her coat off as she went out into the hall. He followed her. She hung her coat on the ball of the newel post at the foot of the stairs, too impatient or jittery to drape it on its usual hanger, dangling from the key projecting from the wardrobe. She went on into the front room, and he followed her there too, as if he dared not let her out of his sight.

30

Then it struck her that this was the crime scene. She stood in the middle of the carpet staring at the armchair she'd found him lying in.

"What was it you were looking at?"

"Looking at?"

He was staring at her in terror-struck appeal.

"That magazine you had. Book. Whatever it was."

"I've put it away," he said hopefully.

"Oh."

She digested this, still not looking at him.

"I want to see it."

"See it?"

His terror was now real, immediate. It pleaded for her to desist.

"Why?"

"Because I want to," she said.

"Well, I've put it away," he said, laughing in a hideous attempt at smug and brutal finality. "So you can't."

He turned on his heel, as on an entire theology of inalienable private principle. He strode into the hall. He went on into the kitchen where the kettle was about to come to boiling point. He paced out the tiny kitchen, pausing now and then to watch the water stir to ebullition through the transparent panel in the side. He was in an agony not so much of impatience as of restlessness. It was a new kettle, a Phillips. The old one, which they'd had for years, had stopped working one day last week. Other kettles were silent until the water within them reached a certain heat, then boiled with a brief noise before switching themselves off. But this one made a noise as of water boiling or seething for several minutes until it actually did boil, which it then did silently for several seconds before it clicked off with a ping.

When it had done, he quickly made tea in the red china pot.

"Tea's ready," he called. Light, casual, too loud.

He placed two cups ready on their saucers with the nervous jerkiness which was afflicting him in all his movements. They were

31

the better cups, Royal Worcester: an offering. He opened the fridge door to get the milk. But then put the carton down swiftly, unpoured. On an impulse of sudden panic he went back into the living room.

His wife had found the magazine in the obvious place. She was turning through it with an odd intensity. The cushion now stood against the upholstered back of the chair. She stopped at one page and stared at it. Then she lifted her eyes to meet his. She closed the pages, as if afflicted with a fury less of disgust than of a brisk impatience. She thrust the magazine into his hands, or rather at his chest, as she went out past him and he clutched it gratefully. She went up the stairs at a quick trot.

"Don't be a drama queen," he called up, imploringly.

She went into their bedroom. The door clicked shut behind her, but was not slammed.

Scorn and bluster, it was clear, remained his sole defence.

"You think other men don't have a wank from time to time?" he shouted up. "The odd hand-job? The old J. Arthur?"

He hung in the hall, listening for an answer, somehow askew in his clothes, like his wife's coat thrown lopsided over the ball of the newel post. He considered going upstairs after her, then thought a stronger option lay in an unregenerate stance. In swaggering defiance, even. A man of strong male appetites, of casual predilections casually gratified, he went into the kitchen and poured his tea. The red china spout rattled against the cup. It was ridiculous. He felt shaky and his right hand, still unwashed, was trembling.

4

The End of the Rule of Beards

It was almost six when his wife came downstairs again. He'd been staring at the tv news. He'd have preferred to be watching MTV, or *The New Adventures of Superman,* Teri Hatcher as Lois Lane. But being found ogling Teri Hatcher, or having to switch channels guiltily, was inappropriate in the circumstances. The news was a sort of alibi. Or like the book you took to read at the dentist's. It showed that you, at least, were not yet at the level of *Hello* or *Autocar.* That even now, as Adorno said, some people were better than their culture.

At the dentist's was what this felt like. Waiting: for his wife to decide to come down and confront him. At any rate, confront the issue. He was sitting at the table, on an upright chair instead of in the comfortable armchair he usually sprawled in to watch tv. That was the chair his wife had discovered him in earlier, and for her to find him in it again now, however innocently occupied, seemed inappropriate too.

His wife looked in from the hallway, but as if in someone else's house, not sure whether to enter or if she was invited to. He saw with a shock of resentful disappointment that she was intending to go to her Keep Fit class after all. She was carrying the holdall with her tracksuit and shower stuff in. She was wearing jeans, her Levi jacket and her new silver Reebok training shoes.

Given what had happened - the sense of marital crisis he had – for her to be going out seemed to him the most inappropriate thing of all.

"Off out, are you?" he said acidulously.

"It's Thursday," she said. "Keep Fit. I'm meeting Mary."

Still she didn't quite come into the room, but moved into the doorway and stood looking at the tv from there. This, he supposed, was a halfway gambit at companiableness. Her face, closed and averted when she'd gone upstairs, now looked almost pertly open.

Together they watched the screen in silence. Troops in dun and wearing turbans or flat hats like Brueghel's peasants stood in the back of an open lorry waving guns, in grim jubilation watching the camera film them. A straggling crowd of pedestrians struggled along a dusty road between hills that looked to be bare rock.

"Kabul has, as they say, fallen" he said, for some reason finding a cheery anarcho-pacifist bitterness an apt political response to the event.

She glanced at her watch, then moved it on her wrist, as if her concern was only that she may have strapped it on a hole too tight.

"Yes," she said. "I was watching it upstairs."

Her hair was combed back. She looked spruce, fresh, neat. Sporty.

But sporty for what? Mary, he knew from what his wife had told him, had a track record; but it wasn't established on the track.

He saw young men in black singlets. Young black men in black singlets. A crowded gym where every activity, every bench-press, stretch or pump re-enacted the acts or attitudes of strenuous sex in which all there foresaw as engaged the more beautiful bodies they were struggling to fit themselves into. He kept looking at her.

"Why not give it a miss tonight?"

She looked too startled. It was almost a double-take.

"Give what a miss?"

"Keep Fit."

He tried to sound implacable, decisive on her behalf. He was still confident that she too knew some form of conciliation had to take place. That they both needed to be exorcised of what had happened.

But when she looked at him her eyes were untroubled, a mild and fearless blue. He saw neither embarrassment nor contempt in them, but something more factual. It was a gaze in which he felt reduced to tiny size, a reflection on the curve of her iris, like a window at the back of a room reduced to a point of lustre on a glazed dish in a Dutch still life.

"Why?" she said.

His only conceivable answer was a sullen and indifferent shrug.

"I told Mary I'd see her at seven," she said.

"Oh, fuck Mary," he said reasonably.

He stared at her, still hopeful he could impose a change of mind.

"So I'd better get a move on," his wife said, looking at her watch again, finding briskness the easiest way out of the house.

Then she was gone from the doorway.

"Fuck *you*, then," he called after her, trying to sound offhand.

He sat staring at the tv screen in an icy, incredulous rage. He listened for the front door to open. Then for it to close. It wasn't slammed. It was shut with a precise, undramatic click.

He waited. He watched the living-room doorway. But his wife didn't reappear in it with a sheepish laugh. He listened. But she hadn't changed her mind at the threshold, and closed the front door without leaving. No one mounted the stairs or went down the hall to the kitchen She wasn't still in the house. The bitch. She'd really left.

He stared at the screen. His mind was seething.

There was a map of Afghanistan, an orange shape on a yellow ground, an irregular, unfamiliar outline like that of an British county. An inset photograph showed the face of the reporter whose voice, the caption said, was coming live from Kabul. The film crew had clearly not yet arrived in this city which the Taliban had fled.

Instead of live pictures there followed the same clip of

Northern Alliance troops heading towards the city, brandishing kalashnikovs from the back of the same lorry, then the shots he'd seen earlier of a young man smiling as he was shaved by another man smiling too, in celebration of the end of the rule of beards. Rolling News, this was called, i.e. day-long repeats, on an endless loop like supermarket music. Meanwhile, the same string of refugees trudged on through a desert so total, so stone-dry and sand-coloured it looked inconceivable that the road or track they struggled along might even link one place to another. It was as if the people on it, might simply be following a course through those bare hills in the way a stream would, if there had been any water to trickle - finding a vector of declivity and least resistance, the wet tongue of its searching for a place to level and pool already bearing dust backwards on its meniscal surface, the runnel of its passage, deepening over time to a shallow stream-bed, a blind trickle downhill, at once inevitable and speculative, a hopeless inarticulate longing for the sea.

It was gone ten when his wife came home, and he'd finished the Bushmills.

It had started with him taking the bottle from the cupboard and swigging a mouthful, what he thought of as a bracer, almost medicinal in intent. Then he'd taken several more swigs, at intervals, back in his usual armchair again, the bottle in his hand. Studying the label as the heartburn cleared. (He noticed that the word "Whiskey" in "Irish Whiskey" had an E in it: an Irish spelling?) Finally he'd stood up again and got a little glass, to submit himself to the procrastinatory rituals of connoisseurship. The nosing, the sipping, the holding up to the light. Spacing each drink. Rather than glugging it from the bottle's neck.

He wasn't a spirits drinker. He thought of himself as a burgundy buff. A savigny savant. A côte de nuits man. And the whiskey bottle had last been opened at Christmas, for visitors. It hadn't been full when he'd taken it from the cupboard. But he hadn't specifically noticed the level. And so, as he came towards the last small glassful, the last burning sip on the tongue, he didn't know exactly how much he'd drunk. At the very least half a bottle, he supposed.

This, though, he meditated with pointless and convoluted pedantry, staring at the empty bottle in his hand, was a question not just of volume but of interpretation. A philosophical question. You might, for example, originally have supposed the bottle to be, roughly speaking, half empty or, equally, half full. According to the truism, this expressed whether you were of an optimistic or pessimistic personality.

Yet, in the case of whiskey, the malt which wounds, both bringer and easer of pain, a truer interpretation would focus on whether you were thinking of the volume in the bottle before you emptied it or afterwards (i.e when it was in you). Thus you might wish beforehand (out of alcoholic greed) for there to be *more* than a strictly measured half in the bottle; yet, having guzzled it, you'd find yourself hoping (out of shame and regret, or in anticipation of the blur and hangover to follow) that you'd drunk *less* than half.

Wouldn't you?

Either way, he'd just drunk half a bottle of Bushmills more or less. And on an empty stomach, as the saying is.

But on a toiling heart.

The pumping-station. Still slowly churning his blood through its gates.

And the more he drank, and the more he went back over what had happened earlier, the shudderingly worse it seemed. A phrase was haunting him, the way words did sometimes, until they became a chant, repeating themselves in your mind like vinyl records used to, when the needle came to a crack to a crack to a crack:

If my right hand offend thee. . .

Then a variant of another phrase about The Wife Taken in Adultery kept pestering him too – was that Biblical as well? And wasn't it the title of a painting? (Rembrandt? Rubens? He couldn't recall the artist.)

But what did that make him?

The Husband Taken in Self-Relief.

Taken. The way a photograph is taken. Seen. Fixed. *Transfixed*. Bare-legged in his armchair, magazine in one hand, john thomas at attention in the other.

And by his own wife's shocked gaze.

He sat and drank and shuddered and gnawed his heart. Until, with the whiskey and the reflexive logic of a person who has suffered a disgrace so great he cannot overcome it, even quantify it, he passed from humiliation to impenitence.

And by degrees to a dulled fury.

For his wife to interrupt him in the full or crescent flower of a personal erotic fantasy was bad enough. But for her to respond by seeing the event (as he suspected she had) as an offence against herself, and their marriage – as a form of infidelity - was worse.

But then not to judge the incident important enough to make her cancel any plans she'd had for going out was intolerable. Unforgivable. It was something, he decided, he wouldn't put up with. Up with which he would not put.

He sat there. He'd drip-fed his anger whiskey till the whiskey stopped. Now he was starting on the gin.

At which point he heard his wife's key scrape in the lock.

He sat there, intent, listening. Waiting, in a rapidly-assumed posture of cold and lordly negligence. She didn't come into the room, but went directly upstairs.

After a minute or two he heard the radio in the bathroom.

It was almost eleven when his wife finally came down again. He'd been goggling half-drunk at *Newsnight*. Jeremy Paxman interrogating some Government stooge on another political scandal. Then Afghanistan again. The same road, the same soldiers, the same refugees, the same young man being shaved. New film of bodies in the dust. They'd been mutilated, the commentator said, but the camera, instead of zooming in on the mutilated parts, drew back. *If thy right hand offend thee offend thee offend thee, Effendi.*

"It's on very loud," his wife said.

She stared at the television. It was the complaint which had brought her down. But the real reason, he knew, was to express scorn and impatience. Actually, the tv was at its usual pre-set volume. The only time it wasn't was when she was out of the room and he switched it silent at the *Mute* button so he could watch a girl group or the background dancers on MTV without her hearing the changeover.

She stood arms folded, peering at him. She was wearing her glasses.

"You've finished the whiskey, I see," she said. "And now you're drinking my bloody gin!"

There was a cold querulousness in her voice. Then she was gone, with a flounce. Up to this moment she'd been careful not to slam doors, but now she did.

He sat there.

It was one of those generalising rages that are cumulative, slow-fruiting, largely retrospective. What infuriated him most was the sight of his wife at the doorway in glasses and her quilted dressing gown. The dressing gown was turquoise in colour. It was made of nylon, and contrived to be both dowdy and garish, as cheap and tasteless items of clothing things often did.

But what actually enraged him of course - as it had done frequently, and over a number of years - was that this drab, this frump in her sensible night-clothes, was the woman who laboured to look chic and stylish when she left for work in the morning, who got up early to shower and to wash and dry her long, thick hair, to stand for intent minutes in front of the octagonal bathroom mirror to put on mascara and eye-liner.

Who wore short, tight skirts, and shiny black tall-heeled boots, highwayman's boots, with knee-flaps and little gilt buckles and rowel-less spurs, just to sit in an office all day or walk down the corridor to the photocopier, but who when she came home couldn't wait to change into something baggy and comfortable, an old sweater and leggings with stirrups and fluffy mules.

Who timed and oiled a tan all summer, shaved her legs and armpits, kept herself in trim. Who went twice a week to Keep Fit classes looking athletic in Sloggi sports bras and lycra shorts and black leg-warmers, and then came home and got into bed with him and the latest Ruth Rendell in pink wynceyette pj's.

A woman who, to look her best for strangers, wore mascara and contact lenses all day, and then at night and in her husband's company reverted to thick-lensed glasses to rest her eyes.

For years, in moments of fury like these, he'd been on the edge of telling her it was time to change her priorities. That she didn't need to worry about looking "sexy" or "attractive" for "clients" or the people in her office. That he, bitch, was the one she ought to be trying to attract.

He stared at the television.

Maybe the Taliban had the right idea about women. Make them wear burqas in public and keep them as concubines at home.

But then, in a moment of icy objectivity, he wondered if they missed out on the eroticism of jealousy.

The only aphrodisiac which, after fifteen years of marriage, seemed to work.

He sat there another hour, working his way down the gin, and staring at the screen. He kept hopping channels, but zapping back to MTV at frequent intervals in the hope of Destiny's Child or some dance video (switching the set silent with the *Mute* button again for Her Upstairs).

Of course, he knew he was being suckered.

He knew that behind all these videos lay a guiding principle of directorial and editorial sadism. The male viewer was aroused by a series of glimpses: of flat brown bellies, of firm brown cleavage, of beguiling smiles or slack-mouthed incitement, of girls with tinsel hair performing some strenuous dance in black leather straps or white thigh boots, a jerking chorus-line of dancers who were the incarnation of your fantasies of erotic domination or submission - fantasies they themselves existed to supply.

But these glimpses were never quite long enough for the eye to settle on, or even fully take in.

Even if you recorded an entire video on tape, for watching later - as he had, often - when you tried to replay it and used the freeze-frame function what always happened was that when you pressed the *Stop* button, a momentary but measurable lag of inertia in the system stopped the tape not on the shot, the girl, the posture you wanted to look at but the next one, the one the editor had cut away to. The purpose of these shots was male arousal, but each one was truncated in the instant of stimulation.

As music videos became more and more outrageous in their erotic content, they represented, he knew, an increasingly explicit form of televised pornography. But it was based on frustration of desire rather than its satisfaction. It was there to invite the idea of masturbation but to deny it easy possibility. The music might provide the insistence of narrative, but the rhythm of the cutting denied the eye the moment of rest it needed to ingest the image.

Janet Jackson, the Spice Girls, Anastacia, Mary J Blige, Destiny's Child, Christine Aguilera - each video was structured around the idea of Girl Power, a feminism gone beyond the rhetoric of liberation to unthinking independence. Looks and money and sheer sassiness had made the new Single Woman confident to the point of blatancy in a sexuality which had become an instrument no longer to entice men but to taunt and humiliate them, reduce them to their secondary biological importance.

That, at least, was the argument. At bottom, of course, it was the same old cock-tease.

And all these tanned millionairesses with their stylists and hair stylists and personal trainers might have been dishier to start with, but at bottom they were no different to the teenage slags and slappers in the studio crowd-shots, or all those bimbolas in bikinis

41

gyrating on a sand-plot in Florida or somewhere in The Grind, hopeless wannabes whose bored body movements and expressions suddenly reanimated every time the floundering cameramen swung the camera back to their part of the beach.

In one of those abrupt, self-contemptuous moments of what he thought of as principle, he switched channels again.

After thumbing round the channels, he found a film on TCM.

It had started, and it was a film he'd seen before. Several times. But it was a good one, an early John Huston, so he left it on, too exhausted and drunk to move now, anyway. He stared at it. He was always telling students how the sign of a good film was that it could bear repeated viewings. Without falling apart. Without even getting predictable in fact.

This - he'd repeated it to a new group only last Monday - was not just because you noticed new aspects of it each time, but because a script sharpened to functional perfection - which in a screenplay meant reduced to as little as possible - and actors who were capable of embodying it with the underplayed, untheatrical skills acting to camera required, made each scene, each moment of the story and revealed facet of character, essential. Instead of seeming a contrivance labouring towards predetermined ends - as a bad film was, even on first viewing - the more you watched a good film it the more inevitable it became.

But *inevitable* and *predictable*, he told them, weren't the same.

He let his eye roam over the rows of student faces, high on his own casual casuistry, developed over years for annual use.

"Let's take an example," he said. "Let's take *The Searchers*. That scene at the end we were looking at last week. John Wayne doesn't have the option of *not* sweeping Natalie Wood up into his arms at the end. Right?

"Him *doing* that is in the script. And then it's there on film. And the film's unspooling on the wheel in the projector. And, once we've seen the film the first time, we *know* he's going to do it. It's *inevitable* he's going to do it.

"But every time he does it", he said, "it's somehow just as moving as the first time. So moving it used to bring a tear even to Jean-Luc Godard's eye, as he famously admitted once. The shrewd and unsentimental eye of a man who knew something about films, and a cold fish anyway, by all accounts. And a guy who, politically speaking, hated John Wayne and every Right-wing reactionary Republican redneck value he thought he stood for. *But every time I see that scene*, he said , *I love John Wayne*."

He let his glance come to rest in the second row, on Claire Tucker's steady, shy blue stare.

"And the reason he does is that, however many times you see that scene, it still astonishes you. Takes you by surprise. Because it's not *predictable*. And it's not predictable because up to that moment the way his part is played, keeps an even *stronger* option open. The option of him not sweeping her up into his arms but killing her instead. Even though she's his own niece. In fact *because* she's his own niece. Because to him, remember, she's been living among Indians all these years, she's tainted now. To him she's just an Indian."

His eye found Kavitha Das's at the front, a plump girl in glasses who was a different kind of Indian. . .

"*Jess a Comanch' squaw*," he quoted, reparticularising the racism and moving into demotic, into transatlantic, a perfect John Wayne drawl.

When he glanced back at her, Claire Tucker's gaze was aglow with admiration. He saw she'd understood his correction, and its delicacy. She'd seen he wasn't just a brilliant and charismatic speaker but was sensitive to others, especially if they were among an ethnic minority. (Yet she knew, too, that he was too alert to the conformities of political correctness ever to use the cant term "Native American". . .)

And in that instant he was certain for the first time, that she understood him and his work the way no one else ever had.

She would, he sensed, be waiting for him in the corridor outside the seminar room, arms folded to hug the notepad and books in front of her: that earnest thin-shouldered posture female students adopted when they wanted to be intellectuals. Leading with the books instead of the boobs. She'd detain him, coyly, shyly, with a question on John Ford's films. . .

And he'd say, "Actually, I was just going for a coffee. . ."

. . . But the film he was watching now was *The Asphalt Jungle*. Directed by John Huston, with the youthful Sterling Hayden and a terrific ensemble cast headed by Louis Calhern as a corrupt but shaky millionaire lawyer and Sam Jaffe as "Doc" Reidenscheider, an ageing criminal mastermind just out of prison after a twenty-year stretch.

It was famous, however, for being the film in which Marilyn Monroe made her screen début - as she did now, distracting him, coming on screen as he sat and watched.

She plays a young good-time girl Louis Calhern has set up in a second property he owns, and who calls him "Uncle Lon". It's one of those parts screen actresses of this period were often required to play. As the kind of woman who wears a satin ball-gown at all times, even in daylight and at home. The one Monroe wears in her small début scene was of a matt sheen, a strapless low-cut *décollété* designed to show to the maximum then permitted the shimmering whiteness of her arms and shoulders and of course the upper slopes of those blancmange montblancs, her considerable breasts.

Guy, though, had never found Monroe sexually appealing, and didn't now. It was something to do with her mattness and whiteness, the slight plumpness under that milky skin. There was a radiance to her, but it was the electric radiance of a lighted set, like city streets at night that have been hosed for the shoot. A radiance that belonged not to life but to black and white Kodak film.

And watching this film now he was more struck, erotically speaking, by a later scene.

By now the brilliantly-conceived but unluckily-favoured heist has turned into a disaster. Two men are dead. Sterling Hayden is carrying the untreated bullet-wound in his side which will drain him like a car-battery until he runs out of life just off the road, sprawled in a field. Sam Jaffe, coolly calculating to the end, is on the run with the stolen diamonds, but a minute or two of weakness proves to be his undoing.

He's a mile or two from the Mexican border, has just finished filling up with petrol, and then gone into the roadside diner. Sitting there with his last drink on American soil, he's mesmerised by a teenage girl. She's jiving to music on the jukebox, and he watches her in wondering fascination. The old man's just finished a long spell in prison, but it's not a lecher's gaze. It's just that this kind of music and way of dancing are provocatively new to him. This young girl's energetic confidence in her own sexuality is more flagrant than anything he's seen before.

And it's enough to lead him to his first and final error. . .

He's on his feet, he's on his way out to the waiting car, his gas-tank's full. He's about to make the last stage of his journey to another life beyond the law. . . Mexico and freedom and retired ease lie just a few miles down the road.

But then the music stops, the dancing ceases - the teenage girl and her bit-part boyfriend are out of money for the jukebox. But Doc's a nice old guy, so he stops, changes a dollar-bill to nickels, gives them one.

And then sits down again.

He can't leave till he's seen this young girl dance once more, for him.

The audience are by now inwardly screaming at him to leave, get out. The Doc's a prince, a clean old guy, a regular old gentleman, and by now, at the end of the film, they're all on his side. They want him to beat the rap, make it to Mexico. They want him to have a dark-haired underage beauty serve him his tequilas on the beach, if young's his bag. They know that this delay, the moment of wistfulness or self-indulgence, can only lead to freak ill luck, that it'll all end with chance recognition, and arrest.

And so it proves. When Doc does get outside to where he left his car two police patrolmen are pulling in, on cue, just as the APB on him is crackling in over the radio. . . Homburg and spats or not, he's back in cuffs - and all for the time it takes to play five cent's worth of music on a jukebox. . .

A jukebox is playing in the coffee bar Guy and Claire Tucker are sitting in. But she and Guy are not about to dance. With him, he knows, she wants to be serious. Seriousness, after all, is something she has only discovered through him. Most of her friends, the other girls in the first year like herself, act as if they'd only wanted to come to an art college for the opportunity to meet boys. To go to parties, experiment with E and crack, and fuck.

"Most of the girls here are so trivial," she tells him. "And the boys are worse. They're so callow. Immature. All they think about is trying to get off with girls and getting drunk enough to go up on the stage at the karaoke night at Salami's."

His tolerant shrug implies that perhaps she's right, that he agrees with her. But that's what young men are like. Lusting after girls and getting pissed up, that's what they do. Perhaps he'd been the same himself, once. Or perhaps not. Either way, he's not going to become censorious about his own students. His job, after all, is to teach them, not only by instruction but by example. And their job is to learn from him.

"By the way, it's a Greek cafe," he tells her gently. "It's owned by Greeks. Not Italians. Everybody calls it Salami's. But it's *Salamis*. Which is a place in Greece. There was a famous sea-battle there."

He laughs dryly at himself, his own pedantic classicism, a gilded, gelded youth at Marlborough or Charterhouse, so lightly worn.

"480 B.C., I think it was."

He sees she's not disconcerted by the correction, so tactful has he been. She's gazing at him round-eyed again, with that look of admiration he could almost feel across the seminar room when his eye had found hers watching him from the back row.

But it was time to change the subject. No one likes a smartarse.

"Going back to John Ford, and *The Searchers*," he says. "There's this famous story about John Wayne's performance in it. About when they were shooting the film, and someone pointed out to Ford that Ethan Edwards, the character Wayne plays, wasn't a hero at all. That in fact he was a bigot, a man twisted askew with racial hatred. And Ford said, *Okay. You know that, and I know that. But listen: don't tell Duke.*"

He glanced at her rapt gaze. Everything sounded new or day-old to a first-year - ancient Hollywood apocrypha as fresh as on-set gossip.

"The point being that for Ethan, an old-style Texas ranger, to be an Indian-hater was *normal* to John Wayne. He was playing Ethan's own image of himself. A man who can't come to terms with post-Civil-War America. Whose flag still has a single star, for the One-Star State. And, let's face it, John Wayne's mind was never likely to be clouded by liberal correctnesses anyway. But the man he was playing was a hero, all the same. A *hard* man and an unforgiving one. A man out of his time. But a brave man and a man with ideals, and who is never less than true to them."

Claire is watching him, eyes starry and ashine, and never less than true.

"Which is why - going back to that scene at the end again - when he runs down that sand-scree after Natalie Wood, we still can't be sure what he's going to do. Which is why, no matter how often you watch that scene, it clutches you by the throat. Because, actually, the logical thing for Ethan Edwards to do is to kill her. The *humane* thing almost. Because, as he says, she's been a squaw to a Comanche brave. And to him her life as a white woman is over.

"So when he sweeps her up into his arms and says, *Let's go home, Debbie*, it's not just that he has to say that line. He has to have that change of heart. He has to find that feeling. And he, the actor John Wayne does find it, and is capable of showing it. By that dragging, slow falter in the voice he uses. And that hapless furrow in the brow that in John Wayne always signals both male strength and profundity of feeling."

Her eyes are shining up at him like Natalie Wood's, lit by admiration for so much male strength, so much profundity of feeling, so much wisdom. And by the intensity and excitement he has brought into her daily existence as a student, the way his

47

lectures on film illustrate life and life his lectures, all filtered through his imagination, as a fable is told in stained-glass in a church and illuminated in all its rich colours by the sun you cannot see.

He bends his head to kiss her.

They are in her flat. She has brought him back there. She has asked him in for a coffee, that universal preludial euphemism. But the kettle has boiled its water and switched itself off unnoticed. She is gazing at him. The bedroom is dark except for the streetlight at the uncurtained window. It lights her face like moonlight. Her eyes are dark and unknowable, the set of her mouth grave with the decision she has made. She faces him steadily with the consciousness of that decision. And the dimness gives her enough boldness to reveal it.

She crosses her arms in front of her waist and with both hands takes hold of the hem of her tight black sweater.

"I wanted to be pure as the driven snow for you," she says.

She peels the sweater off upwards, uncovering her body and, for a second, masking her face. Then she tugs it off over her head, tousling her hair. There's a crackle of electricity as it does so.

"You are," he said. "To me you always will be." He makes a weary gesture. "But I'm as wornout as the driven motorways."

"I don't want a boy," she says. "What do boys know?"

Bare-shouldered, bare-breasted, moonlit, she gazes at him, her eyes dark and

"What are you *doing* down here?"

His wife stood in the open doorway. Her tone was accusatory, instinctively.

He stared at her in a sort of startled terror. She'd put her glasses on again to come downstairs, see what he was up to. Instead of Claire's glowing eyes, he suffered his wife's, made small by the thick lenses, and smaller by suspicion. Her gaze flickered over him. Then went to the television screen.

"Do you have to have it on so *loud*?" she complained. "I was actually *asleep*. It's almost *one o'clock*."

She scrutinised the screen resentfully, suspicious as to what he might be watching. Her face was slack and wan from sleep.

"I've got to get up for *work* tomorrow."

Her gaze went over him again, as if assuring herself that this time he was fully dressed. And he understood, with a knife-twist of despair and anger at the heart, that her coming home earlier and surprising him spreadeagled in devoutest concentration, in a man's most private act, had changed them both for ever.

And now she'd interrupted him again, mid-fantasy.

She threw him a final glance, and he shrank in the framed lenses. Then she turned away.

She'd left the doorway. But that look had left him nothing. A cry of fury locked in his throat.

He caught up with her on the stairs. He grabbed her by a bare ankle and pulled her back to him, dragging her down over the treads in a flurry of bumps. He saw her dark bush, pale legs. She screamed in shock or terror, turning onto her side in instinctive modesty, and the unrecognisable pitch of her scream shocked him in turn. It made him pause before the only action he had left which was sufficient to his wife's scorn, the only gesture he had equal to her distrust.

His fists were clenched. But some phrase from childhood about not hitting someone in glasses held him.

He stared down at her. He turned and went back into the living room, leaving her sprawled. He heard his wife scream after him, but this time it had words:

"You bloody fucking bastard!"

He collapsed into the chair, almost rocking it over by half-sitting on the arm. The whisky was pulsing to an ache in his head. It was a rushing in his ears. The moment was past. He thought it was. Then he heard her scrambling at the stairs, as if trying to climb them on hands and knees. And he went out again silently and went up quickly to the landing, and barged open the bedroom door as she tried to close it against him, and went in after her.

5

Gravity

Even within sleep, from inside the crippling 47% proof headache and the longing for total coma, he knew it was late morning getting later, though he couldn't have said how he knew. Perhaps it was the angle of light coming through the curtains onto his tight-shut eyelids or the sounds from the street that had filtered into his dense and frowning stupor.

He also knew he was afraid to wake, though last night's struggles still had only uncertain status, like a torn-up dream.

His actual dreams had been of suffocating fear and bombsite suburbs. He was wandering through a grid of streets that had been flattened by carpet-bombing, then patiently cleared up by those who had once lived there, as in Dresden: an entire suburb swept into mounds, and the bricks cleaned off and re-stacked, neat as they'd once been in the brickyard. Yet there was still an atmosphere of terrible overarching mournfulness, in which people shocked dumb wandered, clutching slips of paper with their old addresses written on.

Then he'd got locked inside a scene from *Torn Curtain*, the Hitchcock film he'd showed his students last term. It was the part where Paul Newman is trying to kill a Soviet assassin, who keeps getting up again and lurching at him, gravely injured but unstoppable, so that Newman, who is playing a mild-mannered scientist, and doesn't have a gun or knife or anything else suitable for the job, has to keep trying some other, manual means of killing him. These events kept playing and re-playing on a loop: a man going down mortally hurt but getting up again, going down and getting up endlessly, to meet another bout of reluctant and bungled savagery, a grisly scene in the original film which would be comic if it weren't so disturbing.

Unprecedented in the long history of glamorised cinema violence – or so he'd told his students - what was chilling in this scene was that it showed how hard it can be, from a purely practical point of view, to kill another human being: an act accomplished finally only in the indignity of both men sprawled out on the floor and Newman forcing the other's head inside the hissing gas oven.
. .

Dimly, of course, he understood that his brain, brutalised by alcohol and returning cognition, was really circling two analogous realisations:

How hard it could be to have sex with your own wife if she didn't want you to. Irrespective of how hard for her you were.

But how a single blow could still her. The way a film stops, freezes. Stills.

Even in mid-air, a blown hat, a bouncing ball. Gravity-free.

And when he opened his eyes and found himself clutching a pillow on the bedroom floor – and he remembered waking in the night, and that again his wife had still been in the bed, still hadn't moved - everything froze again in certainty and terror.

An hour later it was still unbelievable.

Incredible. Literally. A fact he couldn't credit. Give credence to. Take in. Swallow. Buy.

It was one of those situations of such awfulness you cannot conceive it would ever happen, or has. In which all the clichés come home to roost. Finally add up. With a vengeance. It was a film he couldn't wake from. A bad dream in which he couldn't get up and push his way out of the row and leave the cinema.

He went upstairs several times to look at his wife again. As if to see if she'd woken, come to out of her coma - though each time with a little more certainty that he knew she wouldn't have. Dread had set in his heart, stiffening, like cement damp in the bag. At the sight of the twisted bedsheets, the phrase *the stiff, dishonoured shroud,* heard he couldn't recall where, kept repeating itself in his mind. That, too, was on a loop. Everything was, recurring endlessly. Except for his wife. She was outside it.

Then the phone rang.

He ran back downstairs and watched it in terror.

It rang and rang and rang with the peculiar, unhurried insistence of a caller who knew there was someone at home to hear its ring and answer it. It stopped. It started ringing again. Whoever was ringing was now more certain than ever that there was someone in the house.

He lost his nerve. He picked the phone up.

He waited.

"Hello."

"Er, is Angela there?"

He knew the voice, almost instantly. That is, after the delay in which, it seemed, the caller was startled to hear *his* voice.

"No," he said. "She's not."

"Oh."

Pause. He sensed again the fluster of someone who'd expected Angela herself to answer.

"I'm ringing from her office. I just wondered if she was okay."

Guy knew the voice *and* where he was ringing from. It was the unhelpful colleague from yesterday. The office male. Who'd had the languid arrogance to call her Angela. To act as if he called on more familiarity with Mrs Hughes than her own husband could.

"Who am I speaking to?"

"David. David Fry."

The name was given in a breezy voice, but a falter of hesitancy had preceded it.

"It's just that she didn't show up for work this morning,"David Fry went on. "And she hasn't called in sick."

There was a silence.

"No," Guy said. "I was supposed to call in for her. It slipped my mind. She's not feeling well."

"Oh. Nothing serious I hope?"

"No. Not serious."

Another silence, into which he did not elaborate, reminding himself that the caller had no right to prompt him into medical detail.

"So will she, I mean is it likely she'll be back in work tomorrow?"

The voice had regained the confidence of one who presumes, nevertheless, the official right of an employer or superior to know the probable date of her return to work.

"Not tomorrow, no."

"Oh, I see."

Silence.

"Anyway," Guy said, "tomorrow's Saturday."

"Oh yes."

There was another short, rapid silence: short in time but rapid with the urgency of both men thinking.

"So she'll be in on Monday?"

"Monday?"

Guy thought. The day after tomorrow was Saturday. Then there was Sunday. That gave him two more days' grace. If grace was the word. Amazing grace. How sweet a sound. That saved a wretch like me.

"Hello?"

"I can't say when she'll be back."

A pause.

"Oh well," David Fry said, with a dulled morose tone. He saw he'd have to settle for this, and his voice signalled sudden loss of interest. "Tell her we all hope she's feeling better soon."

He rang off abruptly, as if determined to have the last word.

The house was silent. Guy stood and listened to the silence, reconfirming it. All through his brief telephone conversation he'd had the inhibitory sense that his wife, on the bed upstairs, had been listening with a sort of characteristic scornfulness. The dead, he realised in unwelcome premonition, don't go away just because they're dead.

But he put aside this insight, under the pressing insistence of another, and worse.

He stared at the phone. He understood what had annoyed him in the man's tone, what had rankled ever since the telephone conversation they'd had yesterday. Not just annoyed him. Disturbed him, though only now did he concede it.

He felt the knowledge flood him sorrowfully, but with a sense almost of relief.

What he'd heard in that voice was more than arrogance. It was proprietorial. It was justified arrogance, instinct with contempt.

For him. The husband.

Always the last to know.

It was the smug contempt of the lover for that hapless total stranger and unknowing cuckold whose wife he has been shagging.

His wife.

It was for this man that she'd bought her piratical knee-boots. The embroidered Aubade underwear, in oyster and eau-de-nil. The leopardskin-speckled thong he'd found in the washing-basket. It was for him she'd dieted and joined Keep Fit and lain in the sun in the park all those Sunday afternoons oiling herself and reading a paperback in her bikini.

All of it, from fuck-me clothes to tan, had been for him. For David Fry.

6

Bloody Friday

It was afternoon when he arrived in work. He'd driven to the
college out of habit, though with a vague sense that the imitation
of normality forms the groundwork of any alibi. Either way, he
had to get out of the house, and couldn't think where else to go.
He'd missed all his morning's classes, and found that the students
for his 2 p.m. workshop had given up waiting for him in a corridor
outside a locked studio and drifted off. He found some still in
the canteen, but there seemed little point in bringing those few
back up to the studio. Instead he got a cup of coffee from the
machine too and found a place at one of the several tables they
were sprawled around.

"Sorry I'm late," he murmured. "Car problems."

His students - at any rate, the five or six left – were all
boys. The girls had gone. And Ayrton too, the brightest of the
boys, was undoubtedly already back in the computer room, staring
devotedly at a Mac. What remained was a male rump, cohering out
of inertia or some lingering instinct of the gang. As unattractive as
male rumps usually were (to Guy Hughes at least) they sat listlessly,
in grudging indifference to his presence. He couldn't remember
most of their names – for first-year boys it usually took him
most of the first year to do that. He looked at his watch. It was
two fifteen. If you went by the timetable there were still forty-
five minutes left of the period they were meant to have with him,
which would take up to the mid-afternoon coffee break. They,

55

though, having gratefully presumed his absence, felt the workshop was now cancelled anyway by his late arrival. On moral grounds as it were. He felt so too. And he had no intention of trying to round up a full class now. Most of the group - there should have been fifteen or so in total - had probably already left the college building for later classes at another site. Or had just melted away into Friday afternoon, and the weekend. Anyway, for once, he was glad not to see Claire Tucker. It was only just now, in the staff toilets, that he'd realised he hadn't shaved that morning, or combed his hair or washed his face. When he'd caught sight of himself, for the first time that day, in the small speckled mirror over the washbasin, he looked ghastly.

Like a murderer in a melodrama.

A phrase he comprehended the truth of only in the instant after it came into his head.

He'd actually been thinking of the wild hair and facial expression of one of the individuals depicted in *Los caprices* or *Las desastres de la guerra,* those terrible and wonderful etchings of Goya's. What he had particularly in mind was the one of the man who has had his arms cut off and then been impaled on the shattered branch of a tree as on a spike. The way a redbacked shrike impales a beetle on a hawthorn bush. And there was that other, of the man who is being garrotted. Though he couldn't recall if the face he now pictured in that etching was the victim's or that of the other man, who is pulling a noose tight round his neck and implacably doing him to death. . . But, he ruminated, for Goya, with his dark imagination, perhaps it didn't matter. In these defining, ultimate seconds of their relationship with each other, both murderer and murderee would assume the same expression of horrific intentness.

No lover, even in a moment of rapture, stared into the eyes of his partner with such devouring intentness.

He became aware that the students were watching him. One of them sniggered.

Say something.

"Car problem," he said. Had he already told them that? "I

had to call the AA."

Somebody snorted with laughter at the other table, and he heard someone utter in a squealed whisper the words "Alcoholics Anonymous".

Say something else.

"Why is machine coffee always so fucking hot?" Guy Hughes said. The expletive was meant as a measure of his defiance.

He stood the cardboard cup on the table again, holding it carefully by the rim. He'd forgotten to fit the cup into one of the re-usable plastic holders.

None of the students answered. The other table was helpless with suppressed laughter. Those on his table seemed not to have heard the joke, but were not meeting his eye. But did they ever?

"I can remember when this college used to employ proper tea-ladies," Guy said. "Homely pieces, they were. But they made proper tea in a big brown enamel kettle and'd pour it out for you in a proper china cup, with a saucer. Only utility ware, but you always got a saucer. And a teaspoon. No delicacy spared. They'd sell you a buttered scone or a Chelsea bun or a slice of Bakewell tart. They'd do you a toasted teacake if you wanted."

He sat there with an eager expression, as if awaiting a response, then got to his feet. He was aware as he left the table that students were exchanging pointed glances, and there was more sniggering. To them, he knew, abruptly leaving was only further erratic behaviour and, judged in conjunction with his late arrival and deplorable appearance, more evidence that he was enduring the aftermath of a drinking binge.

But they could think that if they wanted, slander being preferable to the truth. The fact was that he'd thought of going up to the Fine Art library on the first floor and finding a book of Goya's prints. He wanted to study a plate of the one he had in mind.

He would have done so, except for meeting Terry Goss at the edge of the cafeteria area.

Terry Goss was Dean of Fine Arts, a post he'd been promoted to at the beginning of the academic year. He was carrying some papers on his way through to another part of the building. But having seen Guy Hughes, and been seen, he had no choice but loiter to speak to him.

Normally he tried to avoid Guy. But now that was impossible.

He signalled to Guy and waited, wearing a grim, restless yet sweetly patient expression which meant he reluctantly had some disapproval to articulate. He prepared the way for this by looking at his watch, then glancing across at the group of students Guy had just left, thus conveying with the wordless economy of a true man-manager that it was not yet 3 p.m., official time for a coffee break.

After Cheltenham School of Art and the Royal College, Terry Goss had started his teaching life as a painter and a maker of experimental films. Gradually the youthful delusion of talent, and the hope of convincing others of it, had deserted him and he'd transferred his professional enthusiasms to computer-generated imagery software and administration. These specialisations meant he was able to spend most of his working day away from the inconclusivenesses and empiricism of studio teaching or artistic production and devote his time to the Virtual Ideal in the contemplation of a Macintosh screen.

"Holding seminars in the canteen now, are we, *Guy*?"

As he increasingly tended to, he pronounced it as a French name. An incidental result of Terry Goss's recent promotion was revealed in the discomfort he now experienced in referring to his colleagues on first-name terms. He'd instructed his office-staff to address him as "Dean", and would have liked teaching staff – his former peers - to use his title too. Fear of open derision or mutiny prevented him from trying to enforce this, but it was clear he preferred a greater formality to exist towards his person, and signalled it by adopting a more formal manner himself. Using surnames alone would be too starkly high-handed; but the familiarity and egality implied by the usual forenames, let alone abbreviations of them, was unwelcome to him. And so Tony Catt became "Anthony", Ron Spicer "Ronald", and so on. Only those whose forenames were monosyllabic or impossible to abbreviate, Mark Howard, Clive Wills, Barry Johnson, were spared these new designations in which a patronising desire for authority posed as ponderous irony. Returning like for like, according to their own level of contempt or inventiveness, Goss's former colleagues had started addressing him sardonically as "Terence", while referring to him behind his back as "Dino", "Jimmy Dean", or "Dingo" - a contraction of "Dean Goss" often pronounced in a supposed Mexican accent and in echo of the phrase "Hey, gringo!", as in the exclamation "Eh, Deengo!", etc.

Addressing Guy was a particularly delicate discomfort for Terry Goss, and not just because he'd applied for the Dean's job too. His name, however, offered a unique variant in distanciation by permitting him to show his cosmopolitanism, and hint at the ruined barn in the Dordogne he was restoring in his holidays, by pronouncing it as *Ghee*.

"What?"Guy said. "Oh, I just got in."

"So I hear," Terry said. (Pause) "I was, um, coming to that."

"Car problem."

Guy stood there vaguely, distracted from his purpose. Where had he been heading?

"Why didn't you phone in?" Terry Goss asked – meaning, why didn't you follow procedure so as to arrange cover? He'd been at a meeting on the other campus that morning and had only just been informed that Guy had failed to turn up for his morning classes.

"I told you. Car problem. Breakdown. I was stuck on the roadside."

"Don't you have a mobile phone?"

" I forgot it."

"Forgot it?"

"I left it at home."

The answers came pat but with a monotony that lacked

conviction. Terry Goss held Guy's stare weakly, yet vanquished it.

"You left it at home. Not much use as a mobile there, is it?"

Terry waited, trying to look implacable, hoping for more by way of explanation or penance.

"It looks bad to have students hanging around the place all morning, not knowing if they've got a class to go to."

"My wife," Guy said. "I had to stay with my wife. She's been in bed all morning."

"Is she ill?"

"Just a headache."

"A headache?"

"I mean a migraine."

"Not serious?"

"No. She gets these. . . migraine attacks."

Terry Goss 's glance had grown sharp. But now it softened. First his car. Then his phone. Now his wife's migraines. It was pitiably obvious Guy was lying, and without flair or invention..

Guy stood there. He couldn't improvise anything else. He couldn't even recall where he'd been heading, other than away from the students he should be teaching. And he was discovering a strange, somehow terrible fact. That it was harder to lie about the dead than the living.

"Does she?" Terry said.

"She had one this morning," Guy said. "The start of one."

Terry Goss maintained a forensic gaze, but now it was shrewd with pity. He knew Guy was lying. But he saw guiltily how awful he looked. Evasive, haggard-eyed, pouchy. As if he'd spent last night at the roadside, let alone this morning. He, Terry, had himself once struggled to combine a teaching career and a heavy drinking pastime, and he knew the signs. And why wouldn't Guy drink? A mediocre, largely unpopular teacher — yet who got passed over on Peter Principle promotions such as Terry's - and a practising artist of little distinction even in a profession where there were many who used a hobbyist's small talent as an academic credential. You didn't need talent for art, of course. Publicity was what counted. But Guy didn't have the flair to attract it. And his painting style, despite its flaunted irrealities, was still largely representational, a category where competition is killing, and judgement easier. Ron Spicer, with his usual unfair and baneful wit, had described Guy's last exhibition, hung in the entrance hall of a local arts centre, as "the sort of paintings that get done in prison. Art by lifers".

And of course he had plenty to get drunk over aside from all that.

Anyway, Guy's lack-lustre evasions showed that, whatever was on his mind, he, Terry Goss, was not part of it

"You don't look too brilliant yourself," Terry Goss said in an impulse of generosity.

Guy recognised the opportunity not quite instantly, which made the furtive gleam of recognition in his eye more obvious.

"Actually," he said, "I don't feel too fucking brilliant".

One hand shaded his eyes, spanning his brow against the light like a meningitis sufferer while simultaneously feeling his own temperature.

"I dunno. I wasn't sure whether to come in at all today. Perhaps I ought to piss off home."

Terry Goss saw his inflection of sympathy had been a mistake. And he remembered it was Friday, bloody Friday. Home of the Friday Flier. Absenteeism, both of staff and students, was a long-standing problem on Fridays, particularly after lunch. He'd announced in a staff meeting that dealing with this was one of his priorities as new Dean of Fine Arts. All part of Running a Tight Ship. But now, no matter how long the present discussion continued, he already knew it would end with Guy going home for an early weekend.

Terry Goss's pale, fierce, slightly anaemic gaze had faltered with compassion. Now it sharpened again, with fastidiousness, dislike. Why should he waste sympathy on the bastard? Whatever was happening to him in his life, he deserved it.

"Just try to let me, the office and your students know what's going on in future, will you? I don't want them hanging round the fucking cafeteria all day. It looks bad."

"Okay," Guy said mildly, agreeable to the rebuke. After all, he was getting the rest of the day off.

"So you're off home again, are you?"

"Might go and see a doctor, I think," Guy suggested vaguely.

"Get in late, and then off after lunch!"

Terry Goss uttered a bark of acrimonious joviality.

"Hardly worth bloody coming in at all, was it?"

He went on his way, emphasising the stiff, bowed, rangy, scholarly stride he was perfecting, papers tucked high under his arm with donnish awkwardness.

Guy went down to the staff toilets. He didn't feel liberated. He still felt hunted.

Get in late, and then off after lunch.

Makes a man idle.

And sidle.

And hunch.

He went across to look at himself again in the washbasin mirror. His face stared back. It lacked the usual hopeful interest it took in his appearance. Instead it confronted him with sullen doggedness. Or doggish surliness. The expressionless lack of animation of a mugshot still. Or those early physiognomic studies of criminals or cretins.

Yes.

That was it.

It wasn't Goya he was reminded of, not now. What he recalled were the faces of real murderers, criminals of all categories, taken for documentary purposes or identity records. It was a look they had.

Look in the double sense: facial appearance and ocular regard.

It was a look - he realised it for the first time - offered by those who didn't want their photograph taken but were powerless to resist it. That bated stare was the last resistance left in them. An inured and resigned expression which had something in common

62

with the set faces of the dead, the bandits propped on boards, guns in their holsters, hats placed not quite right on their heads. Eyes half-opened even but not looking at anything. Those dark stains on their faces or chests that might be either bullet holes or a grouping of flies.

He stood there, mind pursuing the idea to a series of self-portraits.

Himself, moustached, as Zapata.

Himself, moustached and bearded, as Che Guevara.

Himself as the dead Christ.

A triptych, in fact.

Christ in the middle panel, arms outstretched, but not along the arms of a cross. His arms were draped along the carbine carried like the bar of a yoke across his shoulders, the way James Dean had carried his rifle in *Giant* (and, he recalled, in homage to Dean, precursor of his own acting style, by Martin Sheen in *Badlands*).

The two thieves to either side had been taken down from the cross and laid out. (Barabbas was one. What was the other called?) The three panels were in a painterly style which recalled Kitaj and Bacon. But the depictions largely monochrome tones, hinting at the New York crime-scene photographs of Weegee, that first Ambulance Chaser, who was tuned in to the wavelengths of the police squad-cars and the emergency services, and was headed for the aftermath of the disaster almost before the wail was in the street.

7

The Mirror of Perseus

After parking the car outside the house he'd walked for hours. Parks, outlying suburbs, a council estate, streets crowded with shoppers, along the river.

It was almost dark when he reached his house again. Number 31. This was where he lived. He stood in the hallway. He listened, but he did not look up the stairs. He kept his head averted, as if from a furnace door. Or from an arc-welder, dark-visored, crouched to his blinding star-blue light. Or the way a stunt-double in a film keeps his face turned too steadily from the camera.

He saw himself in these multiple arrested postures, as on a contact sheet or a storyboard. His mind went back to boys in school going abruptly into freeze-frame in imitation of Famous Footballer cards: yelling "Action photo!" - then holding the pose, the still moment in a running joke: balanced on one foot, the other cocked to shoot or cross, the ball imaginary. Somewhere he could hear the cat mewing. He walked through the house and out to the back yard and unlocked the garage he used both as a garden shed and a workshop and called his Studio.

He stood at the bench by the window, in the last light. First he tried doing some quick pencil sketches of the central figure. The two thieves, who hung crucified right and left of the main panel, Barabbas and the other, the nameless one, could wait. For them, anyway, he'd need to look at photographs – Weegee's first of all. You might even call those "candid shots" he thought, i.e. revelatory of subjects who are unaware they're being photographed (i.e. posthumously). Shots of the unlikely and unwitting postures adopted in death by all those all-time losers, punks and hoodlums gunned down on a New York pavement outside some five-and-dime they'd tried to rob, the blown litter in the gutter and the cracks in the broken pavement as bleak and pitiless as Weegee's flashlight and the dark pooling trickle of blood from the head.

He'd also need to look at those taken of the dead Che Guevara brought out of the Bolivian jungle on an old door, in his rebel's fatigues.

And maybe at forensic plates. Stiffs on slabs.

The central figure was what interested him most. This was himself. The martyr whose suffering was an icon for millions. His mind seethed with possibilities. Just as the world seethed under the microscope. Ideas wriggling like germs. Or spermatazoa. Or a ceaselessly glittering sea. The Icon Sea. Beyond the Gutenberg Galaxy it lay.

For the main figure he wanted a foreshortened effect, as if seen dramatically from above – the perspective of the overhead view in the Dali painting of the crucified Christ a-hover in the sky over Galilee. He found that when he stood in a cleared space, not quite under the lit bulb, the shadow he cast on the garage floor gave an approximation of what he was looking for. He stood with a garden rake across his shoulders, arms stretched out along it to either side, studying the shape he made.

But the stylised, identical poses of James Dean and Martin Sheen - wrists hung loosely over both ends of the hoisted rifle as along the transom of a cross, hips cocked slantwise in the worn Levis - blurred in the depthless perspective of his own shadow splashed like an oil-stain on the concrete slab. Meanwhile, the twist to his own shoulders recalled a warped torso-shape in a sketch by Sidney Nolan. Which in turn raised, inevitably, the memory of one of the Ned Kelly paintings. The home-made metal helmet worn like a biscuit-tin. The eye-slit like an open letterbox, through which however Ned Kelly's face is not seen, only empty budgie-blue Australian sky.

He felt a pang of an old, familiar despair, which was also a variety of terror. It was the moment when he feared he would never see anything for himself, neither the world as it is nor the pictorial representation it might be transformed into. When he feared that he too was just like - as he said when out of their earshot - most of the others who taught as lecturers in art colleges, talentless bluffers and duffers, conceptualisers and paravails in various media who nevertheless thought of themselves as artists. That just like them, he was adrift among precedents and influences. That as soon as he had an idea for a picture it became an abstraction of iconic precursors - as with this catalogue he had been mentally compiling, pre-existing images of individuals on the run or outside the law.

How far is the Icon Sea?

As far as the Eye Can See.

Why didn't he just start painting and let the marks on the canvas find or impose their own logic? Wasn't that what painting meant?

He took one of the pre-stretched, pre-sized canvases he used to save the trouble of preparing his own. He stood it on the stained easel, slid the block down to grip it, tightened the brass wing-nut. He found a piece of charcoal and stood in front of the blank oblong. Then he closed his eyes and imagined the cruciform figure with raised arms draped along the gun. He opened his eyes and started working with swift, light, strokes of the charcoal on the white linen.

After ten minutes of what he tried to make into spontaneous and unreflective sketching he stopped and considered what he'd done.

As always he saw first the false lines, the weaknesses in execution.

The slant of the hips was wrong. He'd wanted to draw the posture of a man standing with his weight on one leg and the other leg relaxed, instep and knee lifted just enough to tighten the pale-worn denim at the thigh: an insouciant stance the crosswise presence of the rifle insisted was masculine yet which remained sexually ambiguous, as James Dean himself had been.

More precisely, he realised, he'd wanted to capture an erotic quality which Bellini had given to his bronze of Perseus, a hero who carried a warrior's scimitar and had one foot on the Medusa's severed head, yet was no more than a slender and beautiful boy with a knowing set to the hips, and naked except for the feathered hat and sexy little calf-length buskins.

But there was something too pronounced about the stance as he'd done it in this preliminary sketch.

The one leg was braced too strongly, thus over-emphasising the lateral thrust of the narrow loins. It was another posture exaggerated and arrested. The sort of pose dancers adopted in stills or videos. Girl dancers. It was a deliberate incitement.

To what?

To hopeless desire.

The desire of the sedentary male trapped in the armchair for the lithe girl on the video, a trained athlete whose every movement has been calculated and rehearsed so as to reduce him to a state of arousal and incompleteness, the wistful speculation of the wheelchair cripple.

He put the charcoal down and picked out a broad-tipped brush from a fan of them which stood in an old coffee-tin.

The flat board he'd made into palette was nailed through into the handle, like a plasterer's hawk. His right hand, which held the brush, was shaking. The trembling squeeze of paint he smeared on the board was like a premature ejaculation.

He worked quickly, transforming the image he'd had in his mind into a girl, in boots.

Take the number you first thought of. Change it.

Jazz it.

FADE UP ON INTERVIEW SET.

APPLAUSE.

A low table with a microphone stand, two chairs facing each other. One chair is unoccupied. Melvyn Bragg sits in the other. On the instant he looks to camera we cut to his

CLOSEUP.

This is how his programme starts, his turned glance triggering the full-screen

CLOSEUP

of his face. This isn't a man who signals a change of shot by swivelling his whole body to camera like a statue coming to life. Nor does he suffer being caught looking at one camera while another shows him in profile. The whole studio, the entire available craft or art of production for live broadcast, is at the bidding of his eyelids.

The bouffancy and styling of his swept-back hair.

The sheen of his Italian suit in brushed aluminium and nubbly silk.

The nasality of his timbre, that of a man constantly trying not to swallow his own mucus.

THE APPLAUSE DIES.

"Good Evening. Welcome to the South Bank Show."

APPLAUSE.

Melvyn Bragg waits for it to cease. A New Labour peer, an anchor-man intellectual, all over Britain, even beyond the constituency of the arts, his face has the vague familiarity of a soap actor or a man in a long-running commercial. He travels to the United States or France or Italy unknown, unrecognised. But he can live with that, he's learnt he has to, it's the price of achieving in middle-age what he longed for in his early days in tv, another who had risen without trace.

THE APPLAUSE DIES.

"We've got a slightly different programme for you tonight, which is coming lived from the Barbican Centre, London, in front of an invited audience. A different format from what we usually have. And I'd like to introduce my studio guest for this evening. One of our most acerbic cultural commentators. And, even more certainly, one of our very finest visual artists.

"Ladies and gentlemen, please will you welcome. . . GUY HUGHES. . ."

APPLAUSE.

68

Melvyn Bragg stands, looks expectantly left in welcome as the camera pans across the set to where his guest will enter.

The low table, the empty swivel chair awaiting the guest, the screening flats he should be walking out between, the walkway of raised decking in from off-set.

THE APPLAUSE CONTINUES.

No one enters.

THE APPLAUSE BEGINS TO DIE, UNCERTAIN.

Still no one enters.

Melvyn Bragg, waiting, his smile visibly stiffening. For once an unrehearsed camera shot catches his glance towards the producer, a moment in which the studio crew, the huge Barbican Centre audience, and the millions watching on tv share an experience which is simultaneously one of transferred responsibility and vicarious panic.

Still the low table, the empty chair, the flats.

No one enters.

THE APPLAUSE DIES, UNCERTAIN.

Then Guy Hughes appears. He stands in the spotlight surveying the set, his host, the huge crowd in the Barbican. He does not smile. But nor does he seem bemused by the size of the hall, the number of people, the brilliance of the lights. He seems, rather, to experience a moment of grim and possibly sardonic confirmation.

THE APPLAUSE STARTS, UNCERTAINLY AT FIRST, BUT SWELLING.

As if coming to some private act of consent with himself Guy Hughes makes his way across to the empty chair. He sits in it, surveys the audience with neutrality, not noticing that Melvyn Bragg is standing, hand outstretched, to welcome him.

Guy Hughes crosses one leg over the other, swivels experimentally in his chair. It's clear he's perfectly at ease.

Melvyn Bragg sits too. He grins, allowing a rare glimpse of a cowed and obsequious instinct he started out with as a young arts interviewer, but which now reappears only in the presence of the great, the world-famous, those even he knows he cannot hope to impress. With most people, even celebrated people, a confident air of broken-nosed masculinity and the frequency of his own appearances on television permit him to appear masterful, their equal.

"I thought you weren't coming for a minute there," he says.

He laughs, inviting his guest and the audience to laugh with him. It's a skilful attempt to regain an ascendancy he senses he's lost somehow in the presence of this particular guest.

"It's interesting how television is terrified of silence," Guy Hughes begins. "Of nothing happening. Or of something that hasn't been scripted happening. Something unpredictable. Like applause building for a chat-show guest who doesn't walk out onto the set on cue. Who may not even be there. Who may have decided against it and gone home."

"It's pretentious, I know, but we like to think of the South Bank Show as an arts programme rather than a chat-show," Melvyn Bragg says, breezily sure that flattering the audience on its artistic sensitivities will help change a mood of uncertainty he senses in it.

"What's really significant about television, though, is the amount of control it assumes it can exert on anyone who appears on it," Guy Hughes says. "This is because it's the medium which best delivers the fifteen minutes of fame Andy Warhol foresaw everyone as getting, and which we now all actually think we're entitled to. The assumption is that we are all so desperate to achieve our fifteen minutes that, to get it, we'll do whatever we're told to by the tv professionals. Hence the format of this programme. And a whole complex etiquette of appearing on it, patterns of behaviour it imposes on us. Or imposes on you, at least."

Guy Hughes talks musingly, looking outward into the vast auditorium. It's not apparent if he's talking to the camera or the audience beyond it. But what's certain is that he's not addressing himself to Melvyn Bragg – except suddenly, scathingly in his last remark. He's found a way to sideline the anchor-man and communicate directly to the thousands in the Barbican Centre, and the millions beyond it. There's suddenly a tension of intensity in the hall, a bated excitement at the protocols of control and restriction being circumvented by this man.

"Let's stay with fame a minute," Melvyn Bragg says, a slick segue he hopes will put him in charge again. "I mean, you've had a little more than fifteen minutes of it. But not much. Fame came comparatively late to you, didn't it?"

"Fame comes too early to almost everyone," Guy Hughes says. He pauses wryly, timing it. "I mean, okay, the money's handy. Let's be honest. My work's commanding bigger and bigger prices. I'm happy. The gallery's happy. Even the critics seem to be happy."

LAUGHTER.

"But fame itself? All that's got is what you might call nuisance value."

LAUGHTER.

Guy Hughes pauses, looking at the audience. It's clear he's already established a rapport with them, that they're rapt to his every word.

"All the same, it's what everyone wants. It's the modern obsession. No one lies awake worrying about money any more. Not when the whole country's afloat on cheap credit. Credit, the one thing that does grow on trees. Just go out and chop down some more and set fire to it."

LAUGHTER.

"No, instead people lie awake worrying that nobody recognises them in the street. That they've never been on television. They lie there wondering why they're not being interviewed by Melvyn Bragg. They want their fifteen minutes' worth. And they want it NOW."

LAUGHTER.

He stepped back and looked at the painting. It had changed from the crucified male Christ to a girl pinioned to a tubular steel framework. She was bolted to it by a scaffolding-clamp on each wrist, like a handcuff. Instead of a loincloth she wore a pair of half-unbuttoned denim shorts. Except for the shorts, the clamps and her cross-laced white thigh-length boots, she was naked. The dark patch of her pubic bush, glimpsed through the gaping shorts, was shaved in the shape of a heart.

Changing brushes and stepping back to the painting he worked on quickly.

Then again stood back.

The crotch of her shorts had been transfixed by an arrow, upslanted, buried to the flights. The girl's thrown-back head recalled similar images of Saint Sebastian bound to his stake, or Bernini's Saint Teresa prostrate before the mystic, phallic arrow-shaft of faith, suffering the throes of death and the transports of unholy joy.

The agony and the ecstasy
The pride and the passion
The power and the glory
The coming and the going
The coming both together
For ever and ever
World with end
Amen.

8

Mr. X

He went across the landing into his study, head down, a man walking in a dust-storm without shading his eyes. In this manner he again avoided looking at the closed bedroom door.

He found the magazine he wanted, among the folders and files in the third drawer of the metal filing cabinet. Then he found the girl he wanted, and the picture of her.

He wasn't sure why she, out of all of them, should have come into his mind. At that time, in just that posture. But the erotic instinct, he'd read, was most compelling at times of danger or insecurity. This was only an apparent paradox. In fact it was logical. It was evolutionary necessity. It was at such times that the continuation of the species was most at risk.

She was looking back invitingly over her right shoulder, pale buttocks in the air and the fingers of her right hand parting the narrow isthmus of lime-green silk between her legs. This exposed the furred slit with frankness but it was the orifice directly above it, concealed by the creased tautness of the pulled-aside silk, that she was really offering, he knew. The little pink-edged buttonhole. Evolutionary necessity never ceased, and the continuation of the species had long ceased to be a critical factor on the scale of human erotic imperatives. Simultaneously, in a parallel adaptation, the Sin of Onan and the spillage of fruitful seed - a heinous and wasteful act to a small tribal group of nomads wandering in the desert - had become not only the norm but the ecological choice. In an overpopulated universe, the deviant, non-procreative practice was the responsible option.

He sat down in the chair, and concluded the matter quickly, with gasping urgency. The cat was mewing somewhere, but he was not distracted by it. Rarely had he felt so up for it, as the saying was.

Like a sapling rooted on a slope.

The sort of encounter you dreamt of having with a girl like that. Intense, instant, instinctual, a two-way *coup de foudre* . . .

Naughty Amanda. Now he'd done what she wanted, though, he looked at her with commiseration and regret.

She waited in the same pose, arse-in-the-air, and grossly but for the delicacy of those elegant and skilful-looking fingers parting her own buttocks. She knelt on the rumpled sheets, gazing back at him, still expectant, still coy and breathless-looking. For him. For all of them. She waited like that always. And no foreplay with a babe like this, no seductive build-up, no possibility of second thoughts, no sigh of completion. She never pissed or shat or menstruated. She was self-primed and ready, any time. Flip me over and bone me, she was saying. She was a club that was forever open.

Yet the metaphor embodied the nightclub wanness of his post-ejaculatory tristia. He thought mournfully of the life he found himself imagining for her, on the ambiguous fringes of glamour work, modelling and hostess servicing, of the sessions in drab photographic studios, the bleak hours of early-morning dancefloors and the bleaker ones of early evening bar-tables before the night got under way. The champagne-sale encounters and the mobile-phone assignations, and the showers in expensive unfamiliar hotels, her slender, naked, oft-dishonoured body slipping into the bathroom with last night's or this afternoon's clothing bundled in her hands. The coded names of television actors, professional footballers and politicians in a Moleskine notebook, all the vicarious and tawdry sub-showbiz glitter of a modern courtesan's career.

He put the magazine away again in the metal cabinet. Now Guy Hughes was in her book. The unwritten list of all who had used her without a word of introduction, a club with a big membership: the anonymous legion of the heirs of Onan, whose seed was numerous as sand.

He left the study. And went downstairs, again not quite shielding his eyes against the bedroom door.

But when he reached the hall his glance fell unguardedly on something else.

It was his wife's handbag.

A stylish brown satchel in calf with a single strap and buckle, it stood on the hall table. Why hadn't he noticed it before? She must have left it there when she got home from Keep Fit.

He stared at it. And in a compulsive memory, extinct over forty years, he was taken back to his childhood, to the act of stealing money from his mother's purse: silver coins usually. Florins, shillings, sixpences. He never risked taking a half-a-crown, he shrank from that. He'd though that would be noticed. Small amounts, but regularly, and over a long period, years perhaps.

But what he remembered now was not the coins – and he'd completely forgotten what he'd spent the money on (sweets probably, or ice-lollies, or a Dinky toy car). What he remembered was the intensity of the act of stealing. Of opening the handbag by its clasp - it had a sort of gilt metal cross-over fitting which clipped shut: he could see it even now – then taking out the purse and opening that in turn. An intensity probably unequalled, he realised, until puberty and the discovery of the problem of sex. (Then the discovery of the problem's solution. . .)

His mother's purse was of maroon leather, old and lopsided in shape and badly worn; the stitching at the edge was coming loose. He could see it, as if it was still in his hands.

But what *was* was his wife's brown-leather handbag.

He opened it. He was in a hurry of fear, as he always had been when stealing from his mother, as if she might come in and discover him at any second.

He looked through the purse quickly, but there was only money in it, and some old Visa slips. He thought about taking the money; then left it, out of some inexpressible superstition.

In the other compartments and pockets were various

documents, a bill, a card with the address of a hotel on it, a bus-ticket, a sachet containing a moisture wipe - the kind garages give you free when you buy petrol - lens solution, pens. . .

Then he found his wife's mobile phone.

He held it in his hand. The fear had intensified to dread. He felt asthmatic, he could hardly breathe.

Follow the money, Deep Throat, played by Hal Holbrook, tells Bob Woodward, played by Robert Redford, in *All The President's Men*. But it wasn't the money. It was the talk. Or the talk made material. Derrida was right. Speech was evanescent. Lust craved the pornography of textualisation. It was this. This was it.

He knew this was it.

The phone was on, the screen showing a clock. There were four unread text messages and one opened one in his wife's Inbox. He read them in succession.

PLEASE GET IN TOUCH???!!!.

Are you alright?

What's ahppening?

Are you feeling better?

Missing you already & your XXXX

There was no name, no indication who the sender was. But all had been sent from the same number. The message he read last was the only one his wife had seen (the envelope icon showed a flap lifted); the others (showing the envelope with flap still closed) had not been accessed.

He went into the living room and sat down in the armchair. The messages had now sorted themselves into that randomised sequence whose principle you could never work out. But he scrolled again through them again to find the times and dates sent, and saw that the opened one had been chronologically first. The unopened ones had then accumulated in order. The true sequence, therefore, started with:

Missing you already & your XXXX

His wife had read that, and perhaps even answered it (though there was no message saved in her Outbox). This message, he saw, had been sent at 22:54:03 on the 17th. That was on Thursday night. At just around the time his wife had got back. From Keep Fit.

With Mary.

Or rather, with the man who had sent her the message.

Who, an hour or half an hour after they'd separated, had sent her a message telling her how he missed her already.

Her and her XXXX.

Guy stared at the four capital exes. An advertiser's logo for Castlemaine beer, sponsor of the Australian cricket team. Or the symbol of four kisses.

He missed her kisses.

And the four-letter words the exes jokingly censored.

Her FUCK.

The capital fuck she was.

And her CUNT.

He missed her cunt, the cunt.

The rest of the messages she had never seen. They were sent to find out how she was, why she wasn't in work on the Friday morning, enquiries building up all day, concern increasing to CAPITALS on Saturday after she'd still failed to reply.

Are you feeling better?

What's ahppening?

Are you alright?

PLEASE GET IN TOUCH???!!!

They were all unsigned. But Guy knew who Mr. X was. Now the whole thing was certain. This was it.

Guy was quite calm. Dead calm. This was it. All you had to follow, all you ever had to follow, was the sex.

The mobile phone was still in his hand. He looked at it. Would more messages come? He switched it off. He didn't want to know any more. He went back up the stairs halfway, then stopped. His head was just above the level of the landing. He stared sorrowfully up between the bannisters, at the closed door of his bedroom. But he didn't go any higher. He didn't want to open that door. It was the door that opens in the back of a wardrobe or between the roots of an oaktree, a door into another world, another dimension.

He didn't want to open that door. He knew what the dimension was.

David Fry had sent her four X's. Now she lay in that bedroom, David Fry's ex-mistress. Guy's ex-wife.

9

Face to Face

The senior policeman - a detective, a Detective Inspector, in fact - sat opposite him at the table in the drab interview room. That was what it said on a plaque on the outside of the closed door: "Interview Room".

The Detective Inspector - Dexter was his name: D.I. Roland Dexter – was a grey-haired man in a cheap, unpressed grey suit with a diagonally-striped polyester tie of no known school or regiment. A tall man, imposing when he stood up straight, he looked shorter when seated, as if his height lay predominantly in leg-length. Though it was also true that he sat with a hunched posture. A predatory hunch, like a hawk on a post. He had hooded blue eyes, in which a frosted smile seemed to glitter at times. He was going through a black notebook in deliberately unhurried fashion. He looked amused, in a baffled way, as if he'd searched the book for a note he knew he'd made but now couldn't find, and was reduced to turning every page with special care, rubbing it between finger and thumb to ensure two weren't stuck together.

The other policeman, in uniform, stood watching in the classic stance: feet apart, hands coupled behind his back. The universal anonymous and acneous raw constable, he had a self-important air. Being told to attend at the grilling of a suspect felt like promotion to him. In fact he was there because he was dispensable, the one in the station force most easily freed from other duties.

A tape recorder was positioned on one side of the table, equidistant from the two seated men, and Dexter, closing his notebook as if he still hadn't found what he was looking for in it, suddenly pressed one of its switches. The spools started turning and recording.

"This is Chief Inspector Roland Dexter conducting this interview. Also present is Constable. . . ?"

He paused and fixed his constable with an exasperated look as if steadfastly denied the answer to a simple question, which he was now forced to put again. In fact this was the first time he'd spoken to his colleague.

"Summers," the young man hastened to supply. "Andy Summers."

D.I. Dexter repeated both names for the machine. Then glanced at his wrist-watch, completing the formalities by stating the date and time, all in the same distasteful, lacklustre tone.

Then his hooded lids lifted, and the frosty blue gaze. He looked at the man seated opposite him. Was this the first time he'd met his eye?

"Name?"

The suspect, who had been watching this procedure with the air of an interested onlooker, looked back with an expression that might have been languidly ironic.

"Would you state your full name, please, sir."

"My name? Guy Anthony Hughes."

"Can you tell me in your own words, please, Mr. Hughes, what your movements were on Thursday last, the 17th?"

"Thursday. . .?"

Guy Hughes inflated his cheeks and spread his hands to imply the wealth of narrative possibilities open to him.

"Where do you want me to start?"

"Wherever you like, sir."

"At the beginning? Or *in medias res*?"

"Wherever you like, sir."

"At the beginning, then. Let's see. I got up around nine. I don't start teaching until eleven on Thursdays," Guy began.

He paused.

"Actually, no, I tell a lie," he said. "I got up around six.

80

A car alarm had gone off in the street, outside the window, and it woke me up. I got up to look out of the window. Everything looked in order. Anyway, it wasn't my car alarm. My car was parked where I'd left it, outside the house, in full view of the window, And the hazard lights weren't flashing, which they do if the alarm is activated. Actually, I couldn't see any car on which car the lights *were* flashing. So it must have been further down the street. Or behind the trees. My neighbour has these big trees in his front garden. They're Leyland cypresses."

Guy Hughes held his hands a little way apart, horizontal, one above the other.

"It's hard to believe, but they were *that* big when he planted them."

Inspector Dexter looked at the distance between Guy Hughes' hands, then watched the machine for a moment, drily, as if to see how much tape might be left on the cassette spool.

"I've thought of cutting those bloody trees down from time to time," Guy Hughes continued. "At night. That's when you'd have to do it. Or early one morning, before anyone is up. The sort of hour, in fact, when car thieves are about, prowling the streets, looking for parked cars to break into, for alarms to set off. Leyland cypresses are, let's face it, a very forceful species. An antisocial species, even. They've been known to provoke serious disputes between neighbours, bad feeling, even the occasional murder. And these particular ones have got a little big, and do keep a certain amount of light out of my own garden Early morning light, which gardeners tell you is the most important kind there is for growing things. But on the other hand, I don't grow very much in my front garden as I've got it paved. And these trees also hide some of the houses along the street opposite, not to mention the parked cars which line both sides of the street, bumper to bumper, day and night, wind and rain, from shit to breakfast-time. So from that point of view, so to speak, the view out of my bedroom might be said to be improved by having them there. But there's another aspect to them too. Are you a gardener, Inspector Dexter? Have you ever planted a tree? A seedling? The speed at which trees grow and outstrip the space imagined for them is one of the most persuasive perceptions we have that time is passing without our fully noticing it. You look at them one day, and they're bigger than you are. Next time you look at them, they're bigger than your house. It's terrifying. But sobering. Trees give you food for thought. But perhaps you're more a sundial man, Inspector? I can see you as a sundial man. Given your job, I mean. Do you have a sundial? Did you buy it in a garden centre? With 'Tempus Fugit' on it? In reconstituted stone? Is that how you keep a true sense of proportion?"

Chief Inspector Dexter looked coldly patient, as if he was used to obfuscations and delays, and had all day.

"This is all very interesting, Mr Hughes. But perhaps we could look now at events occurring more towards the end of Thursday, on Thursday evening, say. . ."

"Well, as I told you, my wife went out to her Keep Fit class, and I worked in my studio all night."

"You're a painter, I believe, sir."

"Yes, I am."

"And your studio is where, sir?"

"I have a garage behind the house. I use it as a studio. I keep my car in the street. The street's good enough for a car. But only amateurs, Sunday painters, Brixham berets, paint outdoors."

The Chief Inspector's air of patient uncomplaint merely intensified.

"And you were working in your studio all night?"

"And until two or three in morning."

"On a painting, sir?"

"A triptych."

"A triptych?"

"A group of three paintings."

"Simultaneously?"

"I'm sorry?"

"You were working on three paintings simultaneously?"

"In a triptych the three paintings are interrelated. You don't work on one in isolation, any more than you're meant to *look*

82

at one in isolation. I was working on the relationship between the three. Masses. Tonalities. Colour. Shapes. Narrative."

"Narrative, sir?"

"Call it the succession of events."

"Is there a succession of events in a painting, sir? Isn't it just a still moment? As in a photograph?"

"An interesting question. We should discuss it more fully some time. But this wasn't a painting, as I've said. This was a triptych. You have to *read* a triptych. You might, for example, read it left to right. The way you read a three-frame comic strip. Or a book, come to that."

"I see."

The Chief Inspector's patient air had deepened to one resembling martyrdom.

"Do you read books, Inspector. Or are you more a comics man?"

"Perhaps we can return to the succession of events in your household on Thursday night. . . "

Guy Hughes shrugged.

"You asked me about narrative, Chief Inspector. Which *is* succession of events. But not all cultures read events in the same way. Just as they'd don't read books or triptychs or paintings or even still photographs in the same way. The Arabs don't for example. The conventions of Muslim art are quite different from those in what we call the West. The Japanese don't either. Take Hokusai's *Wave*. Do you know Hokusai's *Wave*, Inspector?"

"I'm afraid I don't, sir."

"I expect you do, Inspector. The correct title is *The Great Wave*. It's a woodblock print, executed in the 1830s, by one of the great Japanese artists, and it's probably the most famous and most widely-reproduced print of all time. It's been re-used in dozens of ways. Pirated, you could say. On book-jackets, in advertisements, in posters. On record-sleeves. Even you, Chief Inspector, must have seen it somewhere or other, even if you have no taste for art."

"I didn't say that, sir. . ."

"No, you didn't. And I've been amusing myself by trying

to imagine what you might have on your walls at home, you and Mrs Dexter, I mean. Tretchikoff's blue Eurasian girl, perhaps? An El Cordobes poster? Or a nice little Paul Klee? It's hard to tell. You might be something of a true art buff, a devotee. But of course pretending you know nothing is all part of the stratagem. The Socratic method."

"Socratic, sir?"

"What we call it doesn't matter. We both know it as a tactic. An interrogator's trick. The oldest there is."

Chief Inspector Dexter resisted the intensifying urge to turn his eyes to the large mirror which covered most of one wall of the room.

Instead he looked down at his hands.

The two men who were watching the interview from the room behind the mirror had grown gloomy. Finally, the senior of them spoke.

"Dexter's getting bloody rings run round him," he said with surprising savagery.

The other man nodded without speaking, eyes cold and anxious, mouth pursed thinly.

"But who have we got who *is* good enough?" he said. "That's the real problem here."

Chief Inspector Dexter's gaze couldn't see through the mirror from his side. And didn't need to: he already knew the expression on the faces of his superiors. But he still had to resist the urge to look towards them.

Instead he looked down at his hands. His hands were large and brown from working in his garden on weekends and in long summer evenings, weeding, labouring, tending growing things, planting trees or pricking out seedlings. Their backs were stringy with veins, and black hair grew sparsely, even on the fingers, in the spaces between the first and second joints. They were capable hands, strong hands, he thought. Trees they knew about, and their growth rate. But artistic they weren't.

"Going back to *The Great Wave*," Guy Hughes was saying. "It's apparently a straightforward composition, a straightforward subject. It depicts a stormy sea, with one particularly large wave rising in the foreground. In the distance Mount Fuji can be seen. We know it's Mount Fuji because it's got snow on the top. Mount Fuji always has snow on the top. And it's shown in exactly the same way a helping of custard or brandy sauce is shown on top of a Christmas pudding in *The Beano*. A white, seasonal topping, bounded by the same wavy line."

"I see, sir."

"Amazing how some conventions leap across cultures."

"Yes, sir."

"But my point is that a Westerner looking at the print is reading it differently from the way a Japanese would have read it. Wrongly, even. Because in Japan in the early Nineteenth century, when this print was made, pictures were read not left to right, but right to left – back-to-front, as we'd see it. *The Great Wave* has become famous in the West, as an example of Hokusai's draughtsmanship, as a brilliant piece of visual design. But if you want to read it as a Japanese would have, you need to hold it up in front of a mirror. Try it some time. It's remarkable how the wave instantly becomes more fearsome. The whole balance of forces is changed. In the reversed composition that upreared, foaming wave-crest suddenly looks poised to overwhelm those boats riding at its foot. And now the effect of distance somehow makes Mount Fuji itself look smaller, as if it's menaced by a tidal wave so huge it will engulf it.

"Seen as a Japanese would see it, in fact, it's not just an essay in design, an arrangement of shapes and colours, unified by an admirable economy of line, a line as bare and minimalistic as in a cartoon. It's a tsunami. It's a real, historical tidal wave of the kind that have periodically devastated vast areas of Japan. It's wrecked boats and flooded villages. It's destruction and death."

Guy Hughes paused. The audience in the vast, dark auditorium was silent, dazed by his swelling eloquence. Throats bobbed, swallowed, they were moved.

"It's also," he resumed, "the dark side of the Japanese psyche."

85

He paused, letting the significance of the statement echo, its own aftermath.

"Looked at one way," he resumed, "Japanese culture is about simplicity of line and elegance of form. It's a world of porcelain and silk and graceful gestures endlessly rehearsed. A world where the white space is as important as the black brushstroke. But it's also a world of Hirohito's Imperial army and The Knights of Bushido and The Camp On Blood Island. It's a world of karaoke bars and the Company Man. It's a world of ruthless hierarchy. It's a world where not all rituals are elaborated forms of courtesy. It's a world of ant-like conformism and the homosexual black-leather Motoguzzi fascism of Yukio Mishima, a Samurai and erotomane who committed ritual disembowelment on himself with a flawless steel blade while sitting cross-legged in front of a mirror."

Guy Hughes stopped speaking. He looked down at the angled platform of his lectern. Throughout the hour-long disquisition his words had been entirely extempore, delivered without notes, and with no need for notes apparent. Now he found himself standing in silence in front of several hundred people without even those few sheets of paper to collect, shuffle and dock together to signify that his lecture was over. Or rather had reached this point of rest – a dramatic and pregnant juncture which he would develop or adumbrate, fugue-like, in the further series of lectures which had been arranged at Cambridge, the Sorbonne, Yale, Harvard and Cornell, in this unique tour he was undertaking of all the finest, most prestigious centres of learning in the modern world.

But perhaps this invited audience which packed the tiered rings of the Sheldonian Theatre was simply rapt, stunned with the bewildering succession of ideas. It had been a riveting experience for them to see this shy man, the solitary figure on the stage, giving birth to thought under their eyes, an unforgettable privilege to see the suppleness, subtlety yet certainty of his mind at work, one of the finest of the century.

The long pause extended, as the audience still dwelt on the speaker's final words, so that beyond the glare of lights focused down on Guy Hughes there was a mesmerised, almost a shocked silence of attention.

Then someone began to clap.

Another person joined in.

Then another, and so on, the sound catching like wildfire, joyously, until the entire vast auditorium of the Albert Hall raged with applause, the noise of so many thousands of pairs of hands smacking together until they were sore and, below that, another, deeper sound becoming clamorous, a bass groundswell of appreciative exclamations and the baying of bravos.

THE APPLAUSE CONTINUES.

Guy Hughes contemplates the vast hall shyly, quizzically. He does not bow or show any sign of responding to such rapturous appreciation; possibly he's a little dazzled by the lights.

THE APPLAUSE CONTINUES.

Joining in the applause, swelling it with his own hands, prolonging it even, and relishing it too, as if it were partly for himself, Melvyn Bragg comes out from the darkness of the wings into the brilliant light of the stage, no, not *him* again, it's Jeremy Paxman, yes, Jeremy Paxman coming out, tall, that distinguished, greying shock of hair, that ironic, slightly scathing glance of permanently raised eyebrows cast sideways at the audience as if wryly to comment on the enthusiasm of their acclaim.

THE APPLAUSE CONTINUES.

Reaching the lectern, the pool of light, and the dignified man who is standing there as if this immense accolade is a trial he can only patiently endure, Jeremy Paxman waits. Then he leans towards the microphone and wryly speaks five words into it:

"Ladies and gentlemen. GUY HUGHES!"

THE APPLAUSE CONTINUES.

Jeremy Paxman stands to one side again. Looking at his guest, and resuming and increasing the strenuousness of his own clapping, he encourages the audience to yet another encore of its own.

THE APPLAUSE CONTINUES.

Finally, slowly, the multitudinous clapping dies out and

Jeremy Paxman is able to conduct his guest to another part of the Albert Hall stage where a BBC cameraman operates a fixed-stand tv-camera pointed at two armchairs and a low table on which a carafe of water, two glasses, and another microphone are set. A second cameraman, audio headset spanning his crown, is crouching, ducking in and out of the rim of light, trying angles for closeups with a mobile Super-8.

Jeremy Paxman waits until his guest is seated and the audience is absolutely still, the silence in the vast hall so intent it forms a material medium circumscribing them, like the ringed lights, the darkness, the breathable air (in which, however, almost every breath is held).

"That," Jeremy Paxman begins in typically robust manner, "was a very forceful yet, if I may say, multi-stranded argument on subjects which perhaps don't get discussed often enough. What you were saying about Hokusai was fascinating. I was particularly intrigued by the way you linked him up with Mishima and then, well, (LAUGHS), pretty much everything else that ever came out of Japan, the Tiger Economy, and so on. . ."

"You're very kind," Guy Hughes says: the slightly clipped, almost-exasperated formality of the genuinely modest person, a man to whom the praise of others means nothing. It's also clear that on this occasion Jeremy Paxman is no longer the famously abrasive public interrogator, the inquisitor whom neither fame nor evasion can divert. Here he too is an admirer who cannot quite conceal the extent of his admiration – what in anyone else would be a kind of sycophancy.

"But I don't really want to talk about Japanese art, or Japanese writers, however important all this is. I'd much prefer to talk about *your* work," Jeremy Paxman says. "Your art. And of course your writing. Because - and this may come as a surprise to a lot of people, who only know you as a painter - but I believe you're now working on a book as well?"

"Yes, well, I think perhaps it's one of those things that happen when you get to my age. There's an old saying that once you've passed fifty you have the face you deserve. Well, maybe you have the life you deserve too. . ."

"You mean the success you deserve?"

"Not just the success, no."

"But that's what you have now, in your career."

"Yes, well, I've been lucky. But success is not the only thing in my life. And I haven't always been successful. So it's certainly not the only thing I have to write about."

LAUGHTER

"So it's an autobiography?"

"I prefer to think of it as a collection of reminiscences. I think I just wanted to feel free to dip into my own life as impulse or memory dictated. Sometimes it's the small things, the trivial events, which matter. I didn't want to tie myself down to chronology, the literal succession of actual events. Sometimes fantasies are more important than facts. And in any case, my life has never been what circumstance threw up. If it had been, I'd still be teaching in an art college and living in a semi-detached house in a road full of parked cars. It's what you make of what circumstance throws up that matters."

"And, as you say, your life wasn't always a success. . . "

"No one's is. Life doesn't work like that. It's doesn't just open out into its folds like a fan."

"In fact success, though it did come to you in the end, didn't come easily. In fact it came rather late. . . Why do you think that was? Why the years of obscurity? And then suddenly this international stardom almost overnight?"

"It's already been said. The artist isn't ahead of his time. It's just that - and we're talking about matters of taste and artistic discrimination here - the public is a long way *behind* its time. And that's true of most critics too, I'm afraid – the people who shape public taste. Because the fact is that when we talk of the critics we're talking about a coterie. What's the collective noun for critics? A bevy? A gaggle? An unkindness, maybe? No, that's ravens. . . "

LAUGHTER.

"Critics feed on other forms of carrion. . ."

LAUGHTER

"Anyway, we're talking here about a small group of people, a dozen or two at most, most of whom live in London and write in the London press. They'd make up one of the most exclusive clubs in the world if they didn't all hate each other's guts."

LAUGHTER.

"As well as hating every decent artist's guts, of course."

LAUGHTER.

"And of course, increasingly criticism is an arm of publicity rather than a guardian of taste."

"So what about the literary critics, then?" Jeremy Paxman says. "For example, your book, I'm told, and by those who ought to know, is already absolutely guaranteed to be an overnight best-seller. And it isn't even published yet!"

"No, it won't be out for a while yet. But I'm told advance interest is very high. And advance sales are extremely good. They say there's even some risk it'll outsell the Bible in America. That's a kind of benchmark figure, apparently."

LAUGHTER.

"No, seriously! When publicity finally starts working for you, instead of for your enemies – boy, you know you're made!"

LAUGHTER

"There's even talk of a film deal, I believe?"

"So my agent tells me."

LAUGHTER.

"So who's going to play Guy Hughes?"

"I probably shouldn't say this, but I hear we're talking to Hugh Grant. After all, we share the same initials."

LAUGHTER.

"One of the things that people are looking forward to reading is, of course, the ordeal you went through following the murder of your wife."

SILENCE

"It was a very difficult time."

"How did you cope? Not only with the death. The grief of bereavement. But the fact that you were the number one suspect."

"I suppose the husband always is. Most murders, they tell us, are domestic. So, in the absence of any clear indication to the contrary, you could say I was the natural victim of British justice."

"And in due course found yourself charged with the murder."

"Yes."

"Whereupon, of course, you took the almost unprecedented step of conducting your own defence at the trial."

"That wasn't really planned. It was a last-minute decision, and I really didn't take it until the trial was literally about to open in court."

"How did that come about?"

"My lawyer came out with some idea that I could plead Guilty to Manslaughter or try for a plea of Diminished Responsibility. I realised at that moment that even *he* wasn't convinced I was entirely innocent of her death. I wasn't prepared to let a man who couldn't take my word on a thing like that plead the case on my behalf."

"Nevertheless, you were acquitted."

"That's right."

"And there was a lot of pretty expert opinion which said that you mounted one of the most cogently argued defences and conducted some of the most forensically brilliant cross-examination in British legal history."

"I'd spent a lot of time with the law books. One thing you do get more of in prison is time to read."

LAUGHTER.

"Anyway, once the case was under way I came to realise I wouldn't have been happy at having someone else speak on my behalf on a charge like that. Not even in a courtroom. Not even a highly distinguished barrister. I think every man and woman finally has to take responsibility for his or her own actions and beliefs. Life isn't like in *To Kill a Mockingbird*. You can't always rely on Gregory Peck in a seersucker suit to put the case in court for liberal values."

LAUGHTER.

"Seriously, though, that's a central tenet of my personal philosophy. You can't just hire in a hot lawyer and expect him to put your point of view. You have to do what you can yourself. But I'll give you a tip about juries. Always look them in the eye. Especially the women. After that, it's like what golfers tell you about playing out of sand. The main thing is to follow through."

LAUGHTER.

"Do what you can yourself. Okay, so that's a useful motto. But does this philosophy extend to cinema as well?"

"I don't quite follow you."

"You mentioned Gregory Peck just now. And Hugh Grant. But there's another rumour that when the film version of your book comes out, Guy Hughes might play himself?"

Guy Hughes shrugs, smiles.

"Hollywood's awash with two things. Cocaine and rumour."

LAUGHTER.

"But you're buying a house there. . . "

"I am?"

LAUGHTER

"Who says?"

LAUGHTER

"Well, I have my sources. . ."

"You want to tell me who they are? I'll have the Mob check them out for me."

LAUGHTER

"But seriously," Jeremy Paxman resumes, smiling. "Let's go back to this starring role you might be taking."

"I haven't admitted a thing."

LAUGHTER

"But you haven't denied it either?"

Guy Hughes shrugs, smiles, he is expansive, he is glib, he is dapper, he is DeNiro as Rupert Pupkin in *The King of Comedy*, the audience in the sweatless palm of his hand, one born to the lights, the adoration, the silver threads in his jacket aglitter in it.

"Let's put it like this. They haven't yet made me an offer I

92

can't refuse."

LAUGHTER.

"I believe there's even talk that you might direct it?"

"Nothing's signed. Either one way or the other. All options are open."

LAUGHTER

"No, seriously," Guy Hughes says.

LAUGHTER

Guy Hughes and Jeremy Paxman look at each other and burst into laughter too. It's obvious that they like each other, that they've become friends on the set, and this unscripted breakdown in the normal professional formalities between subject and interviewer reveals it. Yet it's a delightful, entirely natural moment: they're laughing, the audience is laughing, and it's some time before Guy Hughes can resume.

"No, seriously, and I *am* being serious now, there's a long and actually quite distinguished history of films for cinema made by individuals who are already leading artists in another medium. Salvador Dali, for example, who, as everybody knows, collaborated with Luis Bunuel on *Un Chien Andalou* and *L'Age d'Or*. He also worked with Alfred Hitchcock on *Spellbound* - which fewer people know. Dali designed the surrealistic dream-sequence in that film, for example. Or there's Pierpaolo Pasolini, who first made a name as a poet. He became a film-maker only later. Mind you, he had a good Assistant Director in Bernardo Bertolucci. . .

"I could go on, but I won't. What really matters," Guy Hughes says, "is that there are a number of artists who bucked the system, broke the mould. Who were not prepared to embrace the prevailing styles of narrative or even the underlying financial structures which dominated the cinema of their day, and are still in place in ours. That's what independent cinema has to be about. About avoiding all those Hollywood solutions which boil down to one thing: happy endings. Man Ray, for example, to me is a much more exciting director of films than Nicholas Ray. . ."

LAUGHTER.

"Though I do have a soft spot for *Johnny Guitar*. . ."

LAUGHTER

"Seriously, though, when I think about the kind of film I want to make I do think about people like this. Pasolini, especially. That dark edge there is to his work. But perhaps the real, the primal influence is another painter. Goya. Those wonderful, terrifying late etchings, *los Caprichos* and *las Desastres de la Guerra*. . . And the so-called Black Paintings of course. I want to make the kind of films Francisco Goya would have made if the medium of cinema had been available to him in his incomparable late period, an old man, deaf, in despair, half mad after the years of savage and murderous civil war, with the Exterminating Angel skulking through the streets and Saturn still devouring his own children. . . "

Guy Hughes went upstairs to his study. But he couldn't find the book on Goya he was looking for.

Passing the bedroom door again, again head turned aside, he went back downstairs and out to his workshop, where he found the book almost immediately. It was lying on his workbench. In fact he recalled he'd been looking at it there only the other day. There seemed to be more blanks in his memory. They were intervals of grainy white space in which nothing happened, you were cut off from light and sound, as if you were swimming underwater. Or sometimes he thought of them as wordless bubbles. There was no speech in them, but otherwise they were like the balloon-like bubbles that come out of peoples' mouths in comics. He was a books man, not a comics man. Except for *The Simpsons*. But these balloons of emptiness and silence were not unpleasant. And the silence was not absolute: there was a swirling noise, which was the world flowing past in his ears, again like when you were under the water. Or was it the blood pressure in your own head, the surge of the sea become a whine, the shell pressed to your ear a telephone?

It was a book of Goya's prints. He looked through until he found the one he had in mind. He unfolded his deckchair and put it up in the middle of the floor - because of lack of space in his workshop, it stood flat against the wall when not being used. Then he sat down in it.

The title of the print was *Estragos de la Guerra* ('Ravages of War').

Guy Hughes studied it for a long while.

That the woman whose body was flung backwards across a log or a baulk of timber had been raped before they'd murdered here was indisputable. The splay of the bare legs in death left little doubt. And, even though, for decency's sake, her underwear was still in place on her loins, one breast was bared and other items of clothing had been ripped away. The decency, in fact, was being observed by the artist, by Goya, not by the men who had left her like this. Goya's art was without false pudency or compromise, but pure humanity, the tactful desire to leave this woman a torn scrap of dignity, had caused him to depict the scene of savagery less starkly than a strictly documentary accuracy might have. The woman lay upside down, like an inverted doll – a woman simply tipped up, rummaged and violated mercilessly, so that her head was almost at the bottom margin of the print. Her mouth was open, yet her expression in death seemed ambiguous, as if, once life is extinguished, the throes of agony and sexual ecstasy are indistinguishable.

Another woman lay curled up, her face unseen. And there was what seemed to be a child too, a small figure, also female, and no doubt also the victim of rape. Her mouth was open too, as if no more than asleep, the way a child will fall asleep, head back, mouth agape, at the end of the day. The only male in the picture, the husband and father of the household, lay face down as if he was gnawing the earth itself in grief at what he had endured seeing, although in all logic he would have been dispatched first.

What fascinated Guy especially, though, was the unusual perspective of the work. He'd failed to notice it before. It was as if the scene was being viewed not at eye level but from above, from some impossible viewpoint which overhung the carnage and the whole disordered room and tumbled furniture, the way a light-fitting does. It was like undergoing an out-of-body experience, and looking down at your own corpse. Or, in this case, the corpses of all your family too.

And Guy recalled the scene in *Taxi Driver* (so much went back to *Taxi Driver*): Scorsese again directing DeNiro: the scene where Travis Bickle is mounting the stairs, gun in hand and a lifetime's frustrations and disappointments gathered to a cold homicidal vengeance in his mind. A scene where Travis too is seen from above, and that scene of Scorsese's itself of course, Guy recalled, a quotation from Hitchcock, homage to the famous scene in *Psycho* where the detective Arbogast, played by Martin Balsam, is climbing the stairs in the old house looming above the Bates Motel, and *he* too is filmed from overhead, the camera looking down on him as he mounts to the unutterable shock of what is about to happen next.

Guy Hughes got up from his deckchair, folded it and stood it back against the wall. A lifetime's genius and disappointment was gathering to an image in his mind, perhaps the finest of his generation and yet a beacon to so few. He took a new canvas and stood it on the easel.

Guy worked swiftly, sketching a preliminary outline in charcoal. The woman's body lay spreadeagled on the bed, a victim, her head held at an odd angle which no living neck could tolerate. Her breasts were bare and sagged sideways, like saddlebags. Her bush was shockingly black.

But the man mounting the stairs to her looked strange. Wrong somehow.

The problem was that a man seen from directly above doesn't look much like a man. What did Shakespeare say, Lear on the cliffs, the samphire gatherer on the rocks below, *No bigger than his head*?

Also in *Taxi Driver*, he recalled, Travis Bickle holding the gun out in front of him, a Magnum 57, and you didn't need to be a crazy man to know what a Magnum 57 Would Do To A Woman's Pussy, as Scorsese himself tells Travis, Marty appearing in his own film, the way he liked to, as Hitch liked to, but here playing a husband driven cold and weird with jealousy, a screwball fare sitting behind Travis in the yellow cab parked at the kerb and looking up at the shadow of his wife and her "nigger" lover on the window-blind (the unhinged, quick-talking viciousness ringing true, but a little pat, he, Guy, had always thought, that shadow of two people embracing: pat as the cat in the adage even,. *Two silhouettes on the shade*, like in the song. Those kinds of things were never that cut and dried).

And suddenly Guy saw what was lacking in the picture he'd sketched.

He worked swiftly, mixing oils, squeezing them out from the tubes, using a broad-tipped bristle brush.

When he'd finished the more detailed work he stepped back from the canvas for the first time, to judge it.

Now it had the graphic quality he wanted. All art renders homage to its origins. Here the crudeness of his line and execution recalled the drawings on walls and doors in public toilet cubicles.

Seen from above, the man going under the lintel of the door-frame was now naked, and preceded by his own erect phallus gripped in one hand. Pale-stemmed, violet-tipped, like a horizontal asparagus, it pointed at the figure agape on the bed.

Quickly mixing paints again, Titanium White given a more lactescent touch with the merest smear, of Naples Yellow, Guy with crudeness and brio touched in the leaping gout.

10

The Quick and the Very Quick and the Dead

Guy Hughes woke in the summer dawn, sun slanting in full on him through the dirty window of the garage, splashed quadrilaterals of light. It was this which had woken him. He sat there in its warmth like an invalid, unrested, blinking. It would be a lovely day. Outside the garage, that is. He'd spent the night in the deckchair. It hadn't been a comfortable night's sleep. Much of it hadn't been sleep at all, more a vague, hunted delirium. He didn't know what was hunting him. But he'd retained on waking an ancient terror. That of a cringing mouse for a great white owl, its silent wings barred and immense as the underside of a moonlit sky. An atavistic fear, he thought, from the age of pterodactyls and rocs. (Though had men and pterodactyls been on the Earth at the same time? Or just in *The Lost World*?)

But at least he'd succeeded in falling into unconsciousness – for the last few hours, anyway. He'd tried sleeping just in his clothes at first, but once the gin's numbness wore thin had woken shivering. He'd hunched there, wrapping himself in his own arms. He thought of the blankets on his bed, and the spare ones – thicker-piled winter blankets - stacked in the cupboard in the same bedroom. But he couldn't go into that room. Not at night. Then he remembered the new tartan blanket in the boot of his car. He'd bought it at one of those petrol stations that sell garden furniture, tabloid newspapers, coal and flowers as well. £4.99. A bargain. He had to pass through the house twice to fetch it. "Travel blanket" it said on the wrapper: "100% Acrylic". Its Crawford plaid evoked the traditional luxury of wool and the early days of motoring. Covered knees in open cars and picnics on the downs. He tore the polythene open, and shook out the fringed square of material. Which looked small for a blanket. But, standing in front of the deckchair, he was able to wrap it round his body and upper legs, and so that it hooded his head. Then, like a man clutching his own shroud, he'd sat - jack-knifing his body and letting it go back into the sag of the canvas.

Being tightly cocooned in this way was obviously why he fell into more troubling dreams. Expressionist sequences involving the sheeted dead and huge human chrysalises of shiny chestnut-coloured leather. Faceless and limbless as mummies, they were studded with metal rivets and criss-crossed by straps and belts with metal buckles and other fittings, as in some extreme fashion in bondage wear.

He came back to consciousness with the word "cremaster" repeating itself in his mind, the way he sometimes woke to find a tune running over and over again, over and over again, over and over again, with the bleak, futile insistence of muzak to the girls who worked all day at a supermarket checkout. *Moon River, wider than a mile.* Longer than a night in a ward.

At some point he'd been woken by a car alarm. This, though, was an event which happened most nights, and more often at weekends, and in the day as well. Proximity was what counted. This time the car was several streets away, so the noise lacked volume and urgency.

In fact he'd found its remoteness almost comforting, like the sound of night rain outside a window. Or was beginning to learn to find comfort in it, so that when the noise stopped he was startled. Suddenly it was the unfamiliar silence which seemed threatening.

But for a second or so the noise, like the strange word he'd woken with, continued in his brain, the two-note pattern printing itself over and over on the spool of his audile memory like a motif of roses repeated down unrolled wallpaper.

He found the word "cremaster" again in the flotsam of

memories still washing up from the night, that hangover high tide of scum and rootless weed and rubbish and fearful dreams. *Cremaster*. It was a strange word, of uncertain origin. Wasn't it the hook from which a chrysalis hung itself? A word, then, that meant something to an entomologist.

But to an etymologist?

He'd have to look it up. But then he realised that the dictionary was in the house.

Everything was in the house. Everything he wanted. And everything he didn't want. That was the way they worked it.

He unwound himself from the blanket and stood up straight. He ached as if he'd been beaten. Old age seemed to have come upon him overnight.

He looked at the painting he'd finished in the early hours. Except that a painting is never finished. It is only over-worked, and abandoned.

Towers with arrowslit windows of flesh, bearded with a pubic growth of ivy. A horizon of conical roofs in flame. Wheels slanted on poles. A unicorn with a twisted horn, a red eye, a gross pendent pizzle.

He stared at it with a familiar sense of futility and depression. Goya it wasn't. Or even Bosch. Surreal? It was more mental than arithmetic. And in the morning light the paint had the pallor of colours that are false. White of chicken-feathers, scarlet of coxcombs. Lightless greys. He stood there. He still felt stiff in every joint. And exhausted, as if night was draining him worse than the day.

It was crashing out drunk again, but too tired for sleep.

Which makes a man stumble

And mumble

And weep.

He opened the side door of the garage and stared at the house.

He wouldn't go in there again unless he had to, he decided.

Instead he went along the crazy-paving path and, hidden

100

from sight by the lawson cypress, urinated into the gap between the garage and the back wall of the garden. Over years the narrow space between the old wall of the garden and the newer brickwork of the garage   had become a hiding-place for litter and rubbish, especially broken or unwanted household objects the bin-men declined to take away in their weekly collection, simply leaving the item on the pavement with the emptied bin, in what seemed a rebuke. As if to have taken it away would involve them in some infringement of by-laws. An old kitchen chair with loosened legs and back. A television stand. A rusted barbecue trolley with a missing wheel. A plastic bottle-crate. The old washbasin from the bathroom, with its taps. The kind of stuff you could only get rid of by loading it into the boot of the car and driving it somewhere you could fly-tip it: dump it in some layby on a country road or tip it into the river, to join the mud-stogged Tesco trolleys.

Now, piled or shoved anyhow in the narrow vertical space between the walls, these rejected objects looked almost Braque-like. Or an assemblage, like Homer Simpson's attempt to build a barbecue pit.

Useless and superfluous as they were, though, they had not yet reached the abstractness of abstract art. Each was part of an intimate domestic history. Wherever he looked, wherever he stood to piss, Guy Hughes realised, items from a shared life confronted him in this way, and would continue doing so. Still Life With Absence.

The solution, obviously, was that he must learn not to notice certain things.

Zipping up his flies, his hand felt the mobile phone in his trouser pocket. He took it out. It was switched off. He stared at the blank screen, like a tiny tv's. He thought about switching it on. Would there be any new messages?

What did it matter if there were? Some news he could live without. He tossed the phone in behind the garage wall, heard it drop down among the waste collected there.

After all, he told himself, the artist must live like a hermit. And a hermit renounces the world.

The flesh and the devil
The ring and the book
The jug and the bottle
The sword in the stone.

He went back into his workshop, took the painting off the easel and put another canvas in its place, another idea, still just a few swept-in outlines: work in progress. He sat down in the deckchair and stared at it.

He laboured at the new canvas as at a quarry-face, mostly in dark umbers and ochres, till mid-morning when he felt the urge to defecate. It was not yet urgent, as urges go. (Why would it be? He couldn't remember if he'd even eaten in the last two days.) But an urge was there.

He went to the door of his workshop and looked at the house again. Pissing against the wall was one thing. It was in the Bible even. The Second Book of Samuel. *Whosoever pisseth against the wall.* (He'd been shown the word there by another boy. Graham Smart. He smelt, Smartie. Or stank, Dr Johnson would insist. *You smell, I stink.* From an impoverished, slatternly home, he came to school in the same clothes winter and summer, and always had a sty in his eye.)

But shitting against the wall was quite another matter. Guy would, after all, have to go indoors and make his way up the stairs to the bathroom.

And if he went into the house, he could change his underwear. His trousers, even. He'd suffered an accident earlier that morning. A misfortune, itself defecatory in nature. Shifting his weight in the deckchair, partly lifting one haunch, he'd expelled an easing fart, which proved to be more substantial than that. More of a liquid extrusion. At least this time, though, it hadn't happened in work – as it had a while ago, and more severely. On that occasion - again it was after a drinking bout - he'd had to hurry downstairs to the lavatories, bolt himself in and clean himself up

102

with toilet-paper and the thicker paper towels from the dispenser by the washbasins he'd had the foresight to tear off before going into the cubicle. He'd tried to flush away his befouled underpants, but they'd proved indigestible to the plumbing system. He'd left them in the blocked lavatory bowl for the caretaker to deal with and put his shoes and trousers back on. He'd had to wait till his next free period before he could leave college and cross the bridge into town to Marks & Spencer's to buy a new pair of underpants, or briefs as they were styled on the packaging. Then rush back to college and down to the lavatories, lock himself in another cubicle, and take his shoes and trousers off to put them on. Saint Michael, patron saint of underwear, and all those taken short in it.

He supposed this sort of thing happened to everybody at some time or other. Women occasionally suffered menstrual embarrassments, after all. (At any rate, there were more and more tv ads on the subject - that is, for the sanitary pads which prevented such incidents, featuring model-girls on the shoot or on bicycles, i.e. leading active and exciting lives and wearing white trousers.) And from time to time, evidently, men shat themselves, in this inadvertent, unexpected sort of way. So why did no one ever talk about this? Why did no one relate incidents like that in diaries or autobiographies? (Though Pepys would have, he thought; and may even have done so.) And what was it Poe said? If a man did no more than keep a diary for six months, but were to tell the absolute truth therein, it would of necessity be a masterpiece. . .

A poe was what he could do with out here, he thought, if he was going to spend most of his time in his workshop. . .

Now, though, he needed to go into the house, and quickly.

He wasn't sure how long he'd been sitting in the bathroom before he became aware that the telephone was ringing downstairs in the hall. He'd been trying to find a word for which the forenames "Edgar Allan" would serve as a term in rhyming slang. All he'd managed to come up with so far had been "toe" ("He stubbed his Edgar Allan"). Though racier possibilities included "flow"("Go with the Edgar Allan") or the indecent "blow" ("I let her Edgar Allan me").

Trousers at his ankles, sedentary but roused to agitation, he listened to the phone. It rang with a steady, futile insistence, and continued to do so far longer than any caller usually allowed. From this it was somehow obvious that the person at the other end knew there was someone in the house, but that the call would not be answered. Yet the caller was determined not to be easily outwaited. Letting the phone go on ringing and ringing and ringing like this was a way of letting the occupant of the house *know* that the caller knew he was there.

It was a provocation.

An act of derision, even.

Then, just as the double ring-note was beginning to imprint itself on his consciousness, a pattern of successive tiny concussions, the ringing stopped. It seemed to sound on in his brain more distantly, in an auditory after-image, before vanishing.

He sat there, still not quite giving credence to the silence in the house.

But then, once you'd noticed it, the silence deepened as you listened. It mounted in drifts against the walls, and in corners, on tables and chair-seats and accumulated in the bowls of light-shades, like indoor snow or airborne dust. Except – there it was again – for the cat mewing somewhere. It must be outside.

Guy had noticed a pair of his old trousers hanging from a hook behind the bathroom door. This meant he didn't have to enter any of the other rooms in the house to find a pair to change into.

As he went downstairs in this second pair of trousers the telephone started ringing again, just as he was going past it. The exactness of timing seemed uncanny. Again Guy sensed an insistent, even insolent tone to the ringing, the mockery of any attempt he might be making to ignore the sound. And how did the caller know he was passing the phone at the time?

104

It was with a feeling of reluctance, even of dread, that he picked up the receiver. He felt he'd been blackmailed into doing so by a sinister and unaccountable knowledge of his own movements which it would now be pointless to deny.

Guy put his ear and mouth to the apparatus of dark grey plastic. He listened, but did not speak.

The unknown caller also listened without speaking.

But then said, falteringly: "Hello?"

"Fry," Guy said.

Uttered as it was, this monosyllable could have been either a stated fact or an imperative - surname or verb (in the penological argot familiar from American cinema, as in "I hope you fry", etc.).

"What?" The response was less an interrogative than a strangled note of surprise.

There was another brief silence, only now it was more terrible. Guy could hear it burning along the telephone wire like a fuse, an incandescent hiss. A silence with the intense white light of a magnesium flare in which what could be heard was a realisation in the other man that if his *name* was known, and known so instantly, much more was known as well. *Everything,* even.

"That you, Fry?" Guy repeated the name, discovering pitilessness, an unembarrassable calm.

The caller tried to quell it with a note of hearty briskness.

"Yes, David Fry here. Can I speak to Angela, please?"

It aimed for patronisation, the voice of someone bypassing an intermediary who has come to believe himself more necessary than those he is officiously preventing from conversing.

"She can't come to the phone," Guy said.

"Is she, I mean, is everything alright? I, er, we were wondering in the office here. . . There's something I need to ask her to do with work."

"She can't come to the phone."

"You said that once," the caller said.

An impulse of violence was audible in his voice, as if he wished to clatter Guy's head with this very phone he was holding in his hand – and would have if he hadn't needed the phone to cross the distance between them.

"I just need to have a quick word with her, that's all."

This was said more reasonably, but was still patronisingly insistent, as if the caller thought insistence would do it in the end.

:I told you," Guy said. "She can't come to the phone."

"Is she ill? Unwell? I mean, will she be back in work on Monday? I, we need to *know*. . ."

There was a wheedling desperation in that hanging sentence, that italicised word. Guy realised with a rancorous and futile satisfaction that the man was suffering the uncertainty and grief of passion. A passion which was not so much unrequited as unanswered. He was suffering the Dantesque agonies of the Ignored-in-Love, those equivocal torments in which pique, self-pity, pride and dread struggled for an outcome. But outcome came there none; all that happened was that one or other of those incompatible feelings was activated, then collapsed again into its opposite. David Fry was a man ajerk on those four opposable strings.

He was coming to the recognition that Guy's wife no longer wanted to see him. That she no longer wanted to continue their liaison. (She hadn't called, she hadn't answered his text messages.) And the shocking realisation that Guy *knew* about him too – had known immediately who he was when he rang - only fed this fear. It could only mean she'd told Guy about the affair, made a clean breast of it, promised a new start, repledged her troth, renewed her marriage vows, wept shame and remorse, tears and snot, etc. And that she now no longer wanted to have anything to do with her adulterous lover, her office paramour. Her fancy man. Her bit on the side.

Whatever had taken place between them up to this moment, David Fry was confronting the fact that, inexplicably, without warning, over the course of a few days – and whether out of caprice or whim or principle or wifely calculation - Guy's wife now no longer moistened the sweet part of her knickers for him.

Well, Guy thought with a bleak and futile sense of

vindication, he's fucking right. She doesn't.

And he put down the phone.

He went on into the kitchen. He opened the fridge. There was a plate of cold chicken, scraps and fragments cut from the carcass, mostly the darker meat. It was covered with a sheet of clingfilm. Perhaps it was intended for the cat. But as soon as he saw it he realised he was ravenous.

He didn't have the energy or initiative to make a sandwich. Even if there had been any bread. So he ate the chicken - gristle, skin and all - while standing at the window, feeding the pieces into his mouth one at a time. He was staring out at the garden. But he wasn't really seeing it.

The large marquee was packed. Facing the stage, every chair along the rows of temporary seating was filled with a summery, excited crowd. Many were carrying newly bought hardback books; others had festival programmes. The women wore light dresses and the men were mostly jacketless; but the women outnumbered the men. At the back more chairs had been brought in to make additional rows for extra spectators, many of whom were recognisable as celebrities. A thrilled, eager gossip rose under the light-filled canvas canopy, the hot sun of June filtered out to create a luminous atmosphere of fete or holiday, intense with anticipation and the smell of crushed grass.

Jeremy Paxman, accompanied by his guest, enters through a doorway at the rear of the tent. They're welcomed by murmurous and spontaneous applause from those in the back rows, who spot them first. The two men walk up the coir matting forming a central aisle between the crowded areas of seating. They climb the wooden steps to the stage. By now the applause and anticipation has spread through the entire audience, and swelled in volume, almost to raucousness: it's partly relief: the enthusiasm of an audience whose patience has been tested but is now rewarded. Jeremy Paxman stands at the lectern and waits patiently, with a smile, for the noise to die back. Finally, he has to still it by raising his hands.

"Sorry if we're a little late."

He, looks at his wrist-watch, pulls his characteristic rueful frown, corners of his mouth downturned. Waggles one hand, signalling a debatable point.

"Well, maybe more than a little. Blame the helicopter pilot."

LAUGHTER

Jeremy Paxman's hand goes out to touch the microphone, more nervous gesture than adjustment. He surveys the audience ironically.

"Nice to see such a big and lively, not to mention partisan crowd. For a moment there I thought I was back doing *University Challenge!*"

LAUGHTER

"You're right to be partisan. Good afternoon, ladies and gentlemen. It's a great pleasure for me personally to be here today and to be introducing one of the main events at this year's Hay Literary Festival."

He casts an ironic glance sideways, a variant of the trademark rueful grimace, at the man sitting calmly on the further of the two chairs provided on the stage.

"And it's a great privilege to have been invited to introduce a man who is of course known to you all, that's why you're here. But, reputation aside, I have to declare an interest here. Because this is also a man who has in fact also become, I think I can say, a close personal friend."

Jeremy Paxman looks across at Guy Hughes, who smiles wryly, nods. In fact it's obvious that these men not only like but respect each other, both privately and professionally.

"A man," Jeremy Paxman resumes, "who is not only recognised as one of our finest visual artists but who is now having to be seen as one of the most important writers of our age. I'm not exactly sure what he's going to read tonight, but I think it may well be something from his recently published volume of reminiscences, *Fragments From A Life*.

"I see some of you have already got your copies. I think you're wise, because I'm told they're selling out of the bookshop fast."

LAUGHTER

"Anyway, I look forward to this reading as much as I know you do. I've come to know our guest this afternoon pretty well, I think, over the last year or so, since we first met in a tv studio set where I had the shall we say challenging and unenviable task of interviewing him."

LAUGHTER

"But despite our growing friendship – and despite our also being increasingly involved together in various professional and business collaborations - he's never lost his capacity to surprise me. Through his wit, and through his mercurial artistic versatility as well as his – let's be honest – frequently paradoxical nature."

And Jeremy Paxman throws another sardonic sidelong glance towards his friend, as one who has occasionally been tested to exasperation by both the foibles and firm principles of a man who acts only according to his own rules.

"But of course he's also forced me to think, re-evalute things, confront an issue in a fresh way, simply through his wisdom and his integrity. He's one of the consciences of our age. And one of its iconic thinkers. In a word, a national treasure.

"I could say much more. But what's the point. You all know who he is. Ladies and gentlemen, GUY HUGHES."

The applause swells as the seated man stands, smiling, shaking his head. He makes a demonic face and forms a strangler's hands, which are aimed at Jeremy Paxman's neck. Then plants instead a mock punch on his suited bicep as they pass. He reaches the lectern. He looks back at his friend, now seated in the other chair. Then waits, still smiling, surveying the audience.

"While I was listening to Jeremy there, I was thinking about this quality of likeableness he has. Even when he's grilling one of our so-called political elite . Or especially then. Because nobody is deadlier, nobody grills them to a turn better than Jeremy Paxman. . . "

LAUGHTER

"The fact is, we can still see the schoolboy in him. I think it's something to do with that mischievous expression he can't quite keep off his face. Behind the tv smartyboots, behind the silk suits and sharp ties and the hundred-pound haircuts, we can still catch irrepressible glimpses of the unruly sixth-former we know he must have been: hair uncombed, collar undone, tie half-unknotted. . ."

LAUGHTER

"Okay, he's a little bit of a knowall, this schoolboy. He's a little bit full of himself. But he's full of enthusiasm too, and he's completely unafraid of anyone. He's one of life's natural iconoclasts. . . . And I think perhaps Jeremy and I have that in common."

Guy Hughes looks aside at his friend, smiling, momentarily struck by this novel thought; and the other man nods in vigorous assent.

"But anyway, that's Jeremy, and that iconoclasm is why he's developed into one of our most forensic interviewers, and one of our most fearless broadcasters. One of those people who are essential to the health of the nation. In fact - and he won't thank me for saying this, because he does like be thought of as a tough guy – old Paxo's turned out to be a bit of a national treasure himself. . . "

LAUGHTER. APPLAUSE

Jeremy Paxman sits, one long leg crossed over the other, head slumped between his hands in a mimed agony of embarrassment. His shoulder shake in hidden mirth.

LAUGHTER. APPLAUSE

Guy Hughes stands looking at his friend. Spreads his hands. Shrugs.

"Well, *you* said some awful things about *me* !"

.LAUGHTER

"And what are friends *for* ?"

LAUGHTER

Guy Hughes looks back at the audience again.

"Seriously, though, I'm sure Jeremy was very bright in

school. Well, bright enough to get to Cambridge anyway. But I bet he was also one of those boys who kept it well hidden. Who did all the other things schoolboys are supposed to do, as well as pass exams. Anyway, in that, Jeremy are I, although we're good friends now and have a lot in common, are very different. I mean, I wasn't particularly bright in school. Well, correction. I wasn't *thought* to be particularly bright in school. Or brighter than the average. But then, the averages were pretty low in my school. . ."

LAUGHTER

"And - at that age anyway – maybe that's the difference between high-flyers like Jeremy and the rest of us. He spent most of his time in school trying hard not to look too clever. The rest of us were just trying not to be thought too stupid."

LAUGHTER

Guy Hughes stands there, dapper, smug, milking the applause, for a moment he's Rupert Pupkin again.

"No, I'm serious. . . "

LAUGHTER

"Anyway, I didn't get to Cambridge. Nobody ever even thought of it, with me. For me, the real University Challenge was getting into one!"

LAUGHTER

"In fact I only just about got into art school. . ."

LAUGHTER

"In fact, and it may be a condemnation of our entire system of secondary education, but you see in front of you, ladies and gentlemen, an example of the autodidact. The almost entirely self-taught man. . . "

LAUGHTER

Guy Hughes throws a quizzical sidelong glance at Jeremy Paxman, and shrugs hopelessly, as if to mime "What can you do?"

"They don't believe me!"

"It must be the way you tell 'em," Jeremy Paxman tells him, laughing too.

LAUGHTER

The merriment dies out gradually as the audience in the marquee becomes aware that Guy Hughes, the joking and repartee over, has moved on into a graver mood. He stands, waiting with a patient smile for their complete attention, hands loosely gripping the sides of the lectern. Head slightly bowed, he is staring at its angled plane, though nothing rests on it. Several of the more observant members of the crowd realise he's brought with him neither a copy of his new book, nor a manuscript. No notes, even, not a single written word to read from.

The atmosphere is hushed. Still Guy Hughes waits. He seems to be measuring the silence, even prolonging it, like a played note. It's if he's listening for an inner beat, a pulse, an instinctive sense of timing.

"I was born on a farm."

An indefinable and electric thrill seems to pass through the audience, occasioned simply by the change of register, of timbre in the speaker's voice, the way a great actor on stage, by the manner in which he utters the simplest sentence, can make the small hairs stand erect in the furrow of your nape.

"That sounds romantic. Being born on a farm. Spending your childhood and youth on a farm. It sounds quite rural. The rolling acres of summer downland, home to the rare Adonis Blue butterfly. Cows standing in the river to their hocks. Tudor farm buildings of course, even the barns. All that diaper brickwork. A flitch of home-cured bacon hanging from an S-hook in a beam.

"But it wasn't that sort of farm.

"It wasn't that sort of farm at all. It was more the wasteland at the edge of town sort of farm. The cluster of nissen huts and tarred railway-containers sort of farm. It was more the old bath out in the field full of stagnant rainwater sort of farm. Oh, and the tractor. The tractor that broke down in the yard one day and never moved again. Just turned a different sort of red over the years, from scarlet to rust, because my father was too lazy or too mean or too skint to get a mechanic out to repair it. He spent a day trying to start it himself. Or perhaps only an hour, actually. But I remember standing there watching him. I must have been about seven or eight.

"That was when I first learnt about swear words.

"I can see it now. My old man, with his jacket off, trying to get a broken down old tractor to work.

"That was when I first learnt the wide and versatile application of the word fuck. That was when I first encountered the special rhetorical importance of the word cunt.

"There must have been other words. But not many. Those seemed to be his favourites. And after a while of course they got to be a bit monotonous, a bit repetitive. A bit pointless. Like the noise of the tractor being cranked or the dull whir of the starter-motor when the ignition-key was turned, again and again, again and again, again and again, as if he thought insistence would do it, but the engine not catching. Just that whirring noise dying out into a wheezing noise you get when you know an engine's dead. When the cunt is fucking well fucked, as my old man would have said. Probably it was just the battery which was dead. A mechanic would probably have had that tractor running again in a minute, the old engine shuddering loyally away under its hinged flaps. But probably my old man still owed him from the last time, and the time before that. So this time he had to do it himself. This, I should tell you, was a man trying to get a tractor to work who could barely understand the principle of the wheelbarrow. Or at least maintain one in proper working order, because even the wheelbarrow skreaked when you wheeled it. Skreaked and skreaked and skreaked. Skreaked and skreaked and skreaked, right across the yard. All for want of a drop of oil. And the tyre on it always flat. For want of a bicycle pump.

"That was what happened to the tractor tyres too. They went flat, flat as the proverbial, the legendary, the mythic pancake, and then perished, the way rubber perishes over years. While the tractor turned to rust. The only time it went anywhere was on imaginary journeys when I sat on it, and took hold of that big black bakelite steering-wheel. On the underside it had moulded corrugations for your fingers. I'd sit on it and grip the wheel and try to turn the rusted key that was still in the rusted slit it had stayed in since my old man had given up trying to get it started or had exhausted even the continued usage of the word fuck and the word cunt, used preferably in noun and adjective conjunction, or both adjectivally as in the phrase Fucking cunting thing, said with an infinite variety of tone from enraged and violent threat to a low and bated menace.

"Anyway, that was my old man. And that was his tractor. Which became my tractor. Though no matter how often I sat on it and tried to turn the key, I never managed to drive myself out of there on it.

"Though not for want of dreaming.

"A Fordson, it was. I can see it now. It had a metal seat or saddle shaped to fit the buttocks and haunches, a shallow bowl rising at the front to a sort of pommel. There was a pattern of perforations in it. When it was going – when the tractor was running – my old man would sometimes fold his coat to sit on. No cushion. If it was too cold to take his coat off he'd find an old sack to sit on, or a paper feed-bag.

"That was the sort of farmer he was. And the sort of man. Shithouse rough, as they used to say. Shithouse rough, and twice as dirty.

"And I mean dirty. Every corner of that farm was dirty. Not clean dirt, honest dirt. And not moneymaking dirt, as in Where there's muck there's brass. *Old* dirt. Old filth. Filth of neglect. On my old man's farm muck meant poverty. Squalor. Scaling rust and the fungi of rot.

"And everywhere the scent of shit. Cowshit, Pigshit. Sheepshit. Chickenshit. The yard was awash with it all winter. He reeked of it himself. It was on his boots, on his hands. Under his nails.

"Did he ever wash? I remember him later, in the geriatric ward, when I went to see him again before he died, twenty years after I left home and never went back. I suppose he was reasonably clean then, because the nurses washed him, or the helpers, the ward assistants, or whatever they were called, those middle-aged working-class women with no nursing qualification they employed because they could pay them less. They washed him. Gave him his

114

bed-bath, as they called it. Whisked a flannel under his armpits once a week, sponged his cock, then turned him over, wiped his crack. Like washing a corpse. God help you, I always thought, when you can't wash your own cock.

"Anyway, I suppose he was clean then, more or less. But he still stank. But now he stank of age and piss, instead of rage and shit. A greyish smell, of old skin, lightly perfused with a reek of ammonia. And the stink of institutional food always there too, days-old in rooms where the windows are never opened. In case, I suppose, the inmates take a chill. Or a notion to fling themselves out. It was a prison smell. Of prisoners who would never leave that place. It was the smell of lifers. Of people who are past it all. Who will never now have to change their medication. Or their library books. Or even their underwear, unless someone does it for them."

SILENCE

A long pause. Guy Hughes stares at the lectern as if he's been reading from it and will continue to, though there's not even a sheet of paper with notes on on it. Everything he's said so far has been unscipted and impromptu. Watching his friend with an expression of tragic fascination, Jeremy Paxman is twisted on his seat in concentration, legs crossed, elbow on knee, chin sunk in hand. The audience in the marquee is stilled, transfixed in their seats by the hypnotic narrative power of the man standing on the stage.

"So that was my old man."

Guy Hughes raises his eyes and looks at the crowded rows in front of him, all eyes on his.

"And my mother?

"My mother was a"

PAUSE

"Well, you could say she was a slag. That was the word I heard my father use of her, anyway. It was another new word, if you like. In my growing vocabulary of terms to express rage or voice abuse. I didn't know what it meant, any more than I knew what fuck or cunt meant. What was I? Seven? Except of course

115

that I knew what *all* those words meant. The way even a child of seven years of age does, the very first time he hears them coming from his father's mouth. Because it's not the meaning of the word you understand but the voice it's said in.

"My father called my mother a slag that time in the same way he called the tractor a cunt. It was a special voice he had for moments like that, which were perhaps the most intense of his life. A curious sort of impotent rage which, once he reached it, almost seemed to be a source of private satisfaction to him or even grim amusement, a bitter confirmation of his more usual attitude of sullen ferocity. For a moment he was almost content, in the only way an extreme, a fanatical pessimist can be. When things have finally gone from bad to worse, and he's been proved right all along.

"I don't know what it was my mother had done, that time. Or almost done. Or was suspected of wanting to do.

"But I did know it involved my uncle.

"Not my father's brother. My mother's sister's husband.

"Uncle Reg. His name really was Uncle Reg. He was a sort of dark lanky charmer. A wavy-haired greaseball with a faintly Mediterranean look about him. Or a touch of the gippo, far back. He worked as a manager for an office supplies company, but thought he was Cary Grant. This was the Fifties. People were poor. Worn out by the War. They lived in prefabs or rented rooms, and rode old bikes to work. Men had one jacket for best, and one pair of shoes worth the polishing. Women lived in aprons and skivvies' turbans. A tin of Bartlett pear halves with Carnation milk for Sunday tea was a luxury for the best part of the nation's homes. But Uncle Reg always wore a suit or a houndstooth sports-coat, and drove a beige-and-chocolate Riley with a burred walnut dash and cracked brown leather seats. His fingers were yellow from Capstan Full Strengths, those most manly of fags, a brand-loyalty derived, so he claimed, from his days in the Royal Navy. Though at other times he told me he'd been a commando and had had to kill men with his bare hands or a thin-blade knife. That was what the country was like back then, in the post-War Fifties. Swarming like the Pecos with men with an invented past.

"But with Uncle Reg you were never sure some of it wasn't true. As I say, he thought he was Cary Grant. But he had something of Cary Grant's lean acrobat's athleticism and strength. One of his tricks was to break an apple in half by twisting it in his bare hands. Try it some time.

"Anyway, breaking my parents' marriage in half wouldn't have been hard, I suspect, though I don't know that he had any special interest in doing so, or in my mother. As far as she went, and I think she possibly went all the way, I have the sense a lot of men interested her. At least, I think there had been others before him, or one at least, when my father had been away during the War. I don't know how I came to know that. Something specific he said to her once, perhaps, or just the gist or drift of his unforgivable occasional insults. Or perhaps just a bitterness he had about those years when he'd been away in the Army. He aimed his bitterness at the post-War Attlee Government, and at the historical fact of the War itself. He used the word betrayal, which he'd picked up somewhere. But he wasn't a socialist, or even a Labour voter. Just a man on a slow fire of acrimony at what had happened to him in his own life. A loser and a bigot. And I've come to sense that the betrayal which had damaged him had probably taken place under his own roof.

"Anyway, I don't really know what my mother thought or felt about Uncle Reg. But for me as a kid, with his stories and tricks, he did have a certain wide-boy savoir-faire, a sleazy glamour. In fact I think I probably idolised him. I do know that I wished he was my father. I even fantasised him as my father. Not technically. Not sexually. Not in the sense that I actually imagined he'd had congress with my mother and fathered me. I was about seven, remember, maybe even younger. And of course at *that* point in history, at the point of my conception, he *hadn't* had congress with my mother. That came later, if come it did. Later than my conception, I mean. Though for all I knew he was having congress with my mother at the time that I was fantasising him as my father. In fact that was probably why he was so nice to me on those occasions when he dropped by in the afternoon or my mother and I ran into him in the park, by accident it always seemed. In fact my mother and I might have been idolising him at the same time, chronologically speaking.

"But, as I say I was already six or seven years old by then, and this is all starting to sound like *Tristram Shandy*."

Guy Hughes stands at the lectern. He shakes his head, sorrowfully smiling, as if all this is still a novelty, as if it has an unimaginable strangeness to him. As if he is discovering his own past for the first time in this unrehearsed confessional, which is unpredictable even to himself.

And all the time he stands there the audience waits, silent, unsmiling, utterly intent.

"But the obvious point *now* is that although I knew Uncle Reg wasn't my father, I was looking for a surrogate father. And perhaps this wasn't only because I didn't like the father I had, but because I'd sensed that a stand-in was all he was to start with.

"That even though it wasn't with Uncle Reg, I'd been conceived with someone else.

"In other words, perhaps I'd grasped imaginatively, the way children do, that the man who was said to be my father wasn't my father. Perhaps it was something in his manner, in the way he treated me. Or the way he looked at me sometimes. A look in which many thoughts and emotions might be guessed at, but a sudden welling up of paternal love and pride not being among them.

"Of course, I'm not sure what I felt at six or seven – these things are ambiguous, even all these years later. But I think I knew he never loved me, and never would love me. I wouldn't have known why, not then, but I came to think that perhaps this was because every time he saw me reminded him of something he didn't want to be reminded of. Something that happened even before Uncle Reg came along and my mother embarked on another thing he didn't want to be reminded of.

"It was only much later, though, that I began to speculate on what this first thing was, to piece together hints from remarks my mother once let slip. And from some of the insults my father shouted at her, which at the time hadn't made any sense beyond a generalised rage and recrimination. It was only once you'd sensed where the secret lay, or had made that guess at it, that that the logic of the whole thing, the inevitability of it, shone through the blur of daily circumstance. Weekly, monthly, yearly circumstance. Decades-old circumstance, finally.

"In that sense the story I'm talking about was like a whodunit in reverse, which is the way, or so I've read somewhere, that whodunits are constructed. Crimes get planned by the criminal, and committed, from the motive forwards. But thrillers get plotted from the crime backwards."

Guy Hughes pauses. He pours himself a glass of water from the carafe. The two glass lips meet with a trembling rattle. As it holds the glass, Guy Hughes watches his hand shaking with a sort of curiosity.

Then he toasts the audience, or his own tremulousness, with the glass and drinks some of the water.

Then resumes his scriptless monologue, this impromptu series of reminiscences which at times seems desultory, almost random, yet the intense personal significance of which is somehow clear to everyone listening.

"For most of the last year of the War my father – I'll keep referring to him as my father, despite what I've already said – was in North Africa, following a tank on foot into a sandstorm: cue a blurry shot of infantrymen and armoured vehicles advancing. At least, that's how I've always imagined it - and I've always had to imagine it, since he never spoke about the war or his part in it, perhaps out of that bitterness I've already spoken about and which, again, I never understood until I began to understand what might have happened while he was away to cause him to have nursed such a negative feeling for so long.

"At this stage of the War, with most of the able-bodied men away, there was a huge shortage of labour at home. This was especially true in the countryside and on the farms. I suppose farm-work didn't count as a reserve occupation, like mining or work in certain factories. Anyway, to overcome this, keep producing enough foodstuffs, and so on, prisoners of war were drafted in as supplementary labour. My old man's farm wasn't much more than a smallholding. But some of the bigger farms in the area had men billeted on them as agricultural workers; and some of these men, a small squad of them, came over and did some drainage work on one of my father's fields, which had always been boggy, full of rush and flag iris, and useless for anything except rough grazing.

"I wasn't born at the time of these events, remember. And I only came to hear about all this years later. But I recall the day when my old man started to dig up some of the drains these prisoners of war had laid, because by now that part of the field was boggier than ever.

"I can still picture him kneeling in mud in the ditch he'd just dug and putting his hand up the earthenware drain-pipe where he'd broken it open at the joint. Then he reached his arm in further, up to the elbow, as I'd seen him put it up a cow's arse. He started pulling out half-bricks, fieldstones, chunks of old mortar.

" 'Fucking look at that', he said.

"In the mud there was a scattered pile of all the stuff he'd taken out.

" 'They fucking stuffed all that up it,' he said.

"The pipe, supposedly laid to drain the field, had been deliberately blocked up. I.e to have the opposite effect. A tiny act of rural sabotage.

" 'Still doing their bit for The Fatherland', he said, with that futile and aghast and bitter incredulity he had at any setback. And he stove the pipe in with his spade so that the last act of vandalism was his anyway.

"He said The Fatherland, but I don't actually know if any of the prisoners billeted in the area were Germans. In fact I found out later that most of them were Italian, and he must have known it. So probably this was a way of distanciation. Of denial, if you like. Because once I'd found out more about all this, I started to wonder whether one of those Italian prisoners wasn't plugging something other than my old man's field-drain.

"Anyway, the Italians were only there for the last few months of the war. Round about the same time, my father was hit in the wrist by shrapnel, the wrist was broken, and he got shipped home with one hand and forearm in a long white rigid mitten. There's a photo somewhere of him in battledress, carrying his arm in a sling.

"He couldn't do much work on the land one-handed. But I suppose he could go out in the fields and gesticulate and shout orders to the work-squad who came over from the next farm. Perhaps now and then they came up to the house for something, or one of them did, or had been doing so. Perhaps it was then that my father saw something, or imagined he did: a moment of secretive intimacy between my mother and one of those men. An epiphany. One of those unmistakable but intensely private glances or gestures lovers make when they think no one is watching and because they can't keep their eyes off each other. I've always imagined it as a sorrowful and silent pledge of looks. Or perhaps one hand laid quickly, just a touch, on the back of the other's, consolingly, in mutely mutual regret that, now the husband was back, a relationship was over.

"On the other hand, he might have come home from the village one day and found one of the work-squad and my mother in the act of fornication in the hay barn – or just as unmistakably flushed and guilty after it.

"But, I repeat: all of this is supposition. Speculation. Fiction, if you like. None of these events is known for sure. None of them may have taken place.

"Only two events are certain.

"One is that I was born in January, 1946, and was christened Guy Anthony Hughes. I have never known why. Except that Guy may have sounded like a nice name to my mother, who read romantic fiction.

"The second is that eight months or so before I was born, in May, 1945, three Italian prisoners of war, utilised as forced labour on the farm adjoining my father's land, died as a result of poisoning.

"Their names were Guido Tozzi, Emilio Carbone, and Giovanni Calonzaro, and they were described in a brief report in the local newspaper, which I consulted many years later, as being of 23, 24, and 28 years of age respectively and as originating from the Puglia region of Italy.

"The circumstances leading to their deaths were also stated in brief. One day, while engaged in their routine of agricultural labour, these three Italians had made a soup for their mid-day meal and cooked it on an open fire outdoors, as they were used to doing in their native Italy.

"They'd evidently gathered various herbs and wild plants to use in flavouring the soup. According to the autopsy performed on the men, traces of the leaves of hemlock, which is deadly poisonous, were discovered in the stomachs of all three deceased, this plant having undoubtedly been mistaken for wild celery, wild carrot, chervil or wild parsley – all edible hedgerow plants with which it might be easily confused."

Guy Hughes pauses and considers the vast, rapt audience in the spacious marquee. Somewhere a light plane drones.

"I, I repeat," Guy Hughes continues, "wasn't born yet. Conceived, yes. But not born. And I wasn't told of these events until many years later, and then only through the hearsay testimony of village gossip and in an anecdotalised form which somehow had the effect of investing these three dead men with the temporal distance and stylised outline of a myth. Perhaps because there is something timeless in the idea of these three young men, exiles, prisoners, males in the full vigour of their manhood who find themselves without home or family, and trying to recapture the flavour or scent of their homeland in an armful of wild herbs. I have the sense of three young men whom Caravaggio would have loved to paint, I see them squatting by a fire over which a blackened tin-can is hung to cook a rustic soup. The tin-can has been pierced on both sides, just under the rim, and fitted with a bight of bent fencing-wire. It's a large tin-can, of the size used in institutional catering, and the fire stone-ringed: an impromptu field-kitchen in every sense; and the field my father's.

"There was nothing secret about this story, of course. But I never heard it mentioned in my own family. Which I came to think strange since it was on our land that the event occurred. Nevertheless, I came to hear the story told, or mentioned, by other people in the village. It was part of a locality's oral history of freakish events and prodigies. But stories become remote, as well as familiar, through repetition. And it was more than a decade after first hearing the story of these three young men that I began to examine it in its details. To contemplate, beneath the greenish patination and encrustings of the myth, the appalling immediacy of real symptoms: the stomach pain, cramps, vomiting, sweats, blurred vision, panic, agony by which the three men, singly and jointly, out working in the fields, far from home, and far from any doctor, realise they have been poisoned, and that the poison may be fatal.

"As of course it proves to be.

"And it was only as I started to find out a little more about the three young men than I began to doubt the myth. As for the coroner's verdict of death by misadventure, this was reasonable and straightforward in one sense; but it could also be classed as a convenience of wartime. These three men had no families, and no friends, other than fellow prisoners of war. They might have been nice, pleasant lads and willing workers; but the War was only now coming to its end, and they were still technically our enemies.

"And nothing contrary to the coroner's verdict could ever have been proved, of course, not even at the time. And certainly not years later.

"But all the same, I've come to doubt it.

"I've come to question whether these three young men had poisoned themselves, self-administered, through a mistake. They were countrymen, after all, and hemlock is common all over Europe. If they were used to making soups of wild herbs, whether in Puglia or along the Lugg valley, wouldn't they have known hemlock by sight, and to avoid it?

"I decided they'd been poisoned, deliberately and calculatedly, by someone who also knew the deadliness of hemlock and had put it in their soup. All it took was an instant unwatched and a handful of chopped leaf-tips, almost identical to parsley's; only the plant's speckled stalk could have told anyone it wasn't parsley. Oh, and the smell, the faint sour stench all the books mention and describe as like the smell of mice.

"Nothing, as I say, could be proved. But I became gradually convinced in my own mind that the person who had adulterated their soup was the man I thought of as my father. And that one of the men who died, and who still lie buried in exile's graves in the churchyard in the village – Guido Tozzi, Emilio Carbone, Giovanni Calanzaro – was my actual progenitor. My father, after all – I mean my mother's husband - was a redhead. Very vain of his dark auburn curls, he was. I was always darker.

"Of course, only one person could have confirmed who my father was: my mother. But by this time my mother was dead.

"And, naturally, only my father – my nominal father: David John Hughes - could have confirmed the other suspicion. But he was unlikely to tell me. He was the man who'd killed them, if I was right. If my instincts were true."

Guy Hughes pauses. He seems for the first time to have to consider how to word what he is now going to say.

"One of the things I find hardest to contemplate in all this is the possibility that my father knew that one of these men had been, or still was, my mother's lover and was prepared to poison two other men in order to remove him or exact revenge. That the other two men may have died, in other words, merely to remove a possibility of motive. To create the alibi that all three were poisoned through mischance.

"But perhaps even worse is the possibility that he merely suspected she had had or was having an affair with one of the men, but didn't know which, and was prepared to poison all three on supposition."

"On the other hand I could be wrong. I keep saying that. Nothing can be proved. I can't prove this now. I couldn't have proved it then."

Guy Hughes pauses and takes another gulp of water. He

swills it through his teeth speculatively, like mouthwash, before swallowing.

"Anyway, there's nothing new in all this. It's a wise father that knows his own son. And an even wiser son who is a hundred percent sure who his father is.

"But I've always wondered if my father was Guido Tozzi. And if my name was chosen, by my mother, because it sounds a bit like his. But this, too, is only another guess. In a long list of guesses."

Guy Hughes watches his hand stand the glass with infinite care, as if it's important to place it silently.

"Anyway, I want to be scrupulously fair to this man who brought me up. This uncouth, coarse-mannered, coarse-mouthed bastard I spent my childhood and youth under. 'Under' in the sense that you might spend it as a subject to a tyrant. His work fed me. Clothed me. He never hit me. He never raised a hand to me. And only rarely a voice. But, as I say, I sensed there was something cold at the centre of him, where I was concerned. He saved the brutality for my mother, in word and deed.

"He hit her and swore at her for it instead.

"He hit her and swore at her for whatever may have happened with this Italian and then for whatever may have happened with Uncle Reg. He left me alone. And he kept well away from Uncle Reg. But he hit her. And he called her a slag and a slut. Not often. Just now and then. As if on an ineradicable suspicion that flared up again from time to time. Or when for some reason it struck him afresh that certain things had happened, or might have. Or when the booze took him a certain way. I do remember that. The booze, then his shouting, and her screams.

"But, as I say, if I'm to be utterly honest, I still don't know what it was she'd done or was supposed to have done.

"I'm not sure even he did.

"He may not even have been sure about the Italian prisoner of war. It may just have been the way a young man smiled at my mother once, or the way she smiled at him. Murders have been committed for less. Many times.

125

"It may in fact have all boiled down to no more than suspicion. Jealousy. That greenest, most poisonous of all plants.

"But, for a man like my old man, perhaps suspicion was worse than proof.

"I also came to understand much later that you can know certain things without really going to the point of gaining proof. Some things can never be proved. And some things you don't need to prove. Some things you might even prefer not to prove. Not absolutely. Let's face it, you don't have to hire a detective to know if you wife is a slag, to use my father's word. A slut. You don't have to have her followed. Or follow her yourself. You don't have to go through her handbag. Or the washing-basket. You do. You do all that. But you don't have to. You know it already. You know it from all those signs you can't help seeing, but don't want to see. From the way she talks to other men, or looks at them. Or just one man. From the way she's started dressing herself up to go to work. The makeup, the scent, the underwear, the little skirts. The new scales in the bathroom. And the way she dresses down when she's back home with you. With Him Indoors. With hubbie. The housecoat, the shapeless slacks, the slippers, the glasses.

"In fact you know it even earlier than that.

"You know it from the very first time you fucked her yourself. When getting it into her turned out to be so much easier than you thought. And you knew, right then, that there'd been other men before you. That you weren't exactly the first.

"So why would you, realistically speaking, expect to be the last?

"You didn't want to see these things. You'd have preferred not to. Not to have to think about it. Worry about it. Have it gnawing at you, eating at you. That there was a certain . . . looseness in her. A certain sexual. . . alacrity which was, however, missing now in your own relationship with her.

"But you'd always known that it was there. You'd known she was easy, from the start."

Guy Hughes looks at the audience. They, and Jeremy Paxman, are grave, intent.

126

Guy Hughes lifts his hands in a mild gesture of bewilderment.

"You, and that cancerous worm in your heart."

He stands there in the light, summery atmosphere of the marquee, amid the smell of canvas and crushed grass. A bee has found its way in through the open doorway or a vent in the double-peaked roof: a large, heavy-bodied bee, one of those of which science speaks when it declares that, aerodynamically speaking, bees should find winged flight impossible. It drones over the heads of the audience, seeking a way out.

But none of the audience is leaving. They sit motionless, as if hypnotised. The drawn, concentrating faces of young women. In some of the men, a bated or hooded look about the eyes. It is as if all know whereof Guy Hughes has spoken, but all must stay silent. Yet all, it is clear, are emotionally moved, have been touched in some live, incandescent core of their own experience, and thereby revealed to themselves, through the testimony of the man standing at the lectern on the stage.

It is clear, too, that Guy Hughes senses this. He stands looking back at them. Then he nods, sadly, sagely.

"Some of you know what I'm talking about, don't you?"

Some of the young women nod their heads slowly too, a sad, almost imperceptible movement of assent, as if their own most subterranean thoughts and feelings have been revealed. Some of the men, though, drop their eyes. And one sits holding his head in his hands. His shoulders shake gently with tears.

All have been revealed, and all know it. Revealed not to others but privately, to themselves; and, among those who had come there as couples, to their partners. All their past lives, their furtive lusts or brash flirtations, every promiscuity of thought and act, and every suspicion of another's infidelity, have been exposed. All this has been confirmed, yet comprehended, through the universal humanity of the man on the stage, who has only been talking in a spontaneous subjective retrospective way about his own life.

All who were there have been inwardly revealed, yet all have been forgiven and redeemed.

And suddenly a young woman stands up in one of the rows of seating near the back of the marquee.

It is Claire Tucker. She is wearing a white summer dress of cotton with a simple floral print of roses repeated on it. White and blue summer flowers are plaited into her hair. It's somehow clear that she's forgotten where she is, even that she's in public; that something has transformed her, even beyond the transformations undergone by all the other people in the audience. She gazes up at the man on the stage and, mastering his astonishment at seeing her there, he gazes back.

"I've waited for you to speak," Claire Tucker says. "Since the first time I saw you. Since I first came to your art classes. Began to follow your teaching. But you never did speak. So now I'm going to."

"Claire," the man on the stage begins. "I'm sorry. This isn't the time. The place."

The words are stammered. For once this man, who has held this huge audience intent and silent in the grip of nothing more substantial than the timbre of his voice, seems confused, unsure what to say.

"Of course, I knew you wouldn't speak," Claire Tucker says. "Or felt you couldn't speak. Because you were a married man."

"Claire."

"At first I just wanted you to notice me," Claire Tucker says. "All those times when you stood next to me, stood next to my easel or my sketchbook, looking at my work, helping me with my work. And I did want you to look at my work. Because I wanted to do good work for you. Fine work. Great work, even, one day perhaps, in the way that I knew yours was great. And I even did feel sometimes that I might do great work, with your help. But that was as an artist, or someone who was hoping to become one. But as a woman, of course, I didn't want you to see my work, I wanted you to see me.

"And at home, when I looked in the mirror sometimes, I thought, Am I not handsome for him? Comely? Am I not like a heap of wheat? Are not fine hairs of the finest gold on my neck and wrists and shins for him to see?

"But of course I knew you didn't see them You didn't see me. Or wouldn't. Any more than you noticed the other girls. Half of us were in love with you, and you never even knew it. We never spoke about it to each other, we all nursed it as our own secret. But I saw the way they looked at you, the shine in their eyes. And they must have seen the way I looked at you. Oh, you never saw it. And I knew that even if you did see it you would put it from your mind. Because you were a married man. And because of your sense of responsibility as our teacher.

"But I only admired you more for that. Respected you more. As I'd come to admire and respect you as an artist. And as a human being. As a man of wisdom and integrity. Oh, I don't know, there was this fineness, this nobility about you, Guy. . . But your fame didn't matter to me. It didn't matter to me that you were one of the finest minds of your generation. That you were already one of the men of the century. What mattered to me was your presence. What mattered to me was that you were standing by my easel, looking over my shoulder, all the time I could sense you there, I could inhale your scent, while you were looking at some poor, juvenile attempt I was making to try and become an artist too. . ."

Claire Tucker's words break down for a moment. She is laughing through tears, at her own youthful folly, her own devotion, yet happy in a curious way at having finally confessed to it all.

"But of course you didn't notice me. Or, if you did, you never let me see that you had. You were always so discreet. So in control of yourself. So much a man of principle."

"Claire."

"Of course other boys noticed me. Men noticed me. All the time. Men were always sniffing around. They have been since I was fourteen. I knew that. I knew what it meant. I even went out with some of the boys. Boys of my own age. Students like me. I chose them because I thought it was the normal thing to do, and I thought perhaps it would help me get over you, who I already knew was the love of my life. But I also thought that if you saw me with one of them you might experience a pang of some feeling for me. A pang of jealousy. Like with that boy you saw me kissing in the street that day. I only let him kiss me, I only let him put his tongue in my mouth, because you were there. Was it wrong of me? It seems very wrong now. I suppose I was in some kind of despair by then. . .

"But his kiss left me unmoved. Boys did nothing for me. Nor men either. And I felt filthy afterwards. I felt I'd betrayed you. *Us*. What we might one day become together."

"Claire, please."

"And I knew then that whatever happened, my only choice was to keep myself for you. . . "

"Claire."

The man on the stage is confused, almost distraught. He is for once unable to find the words that will deliver him from the intolerable burden of being. Of being an icon to so many.

"And so I have," Claire Tucker says. "I have kept myself for you. Devoutly. Piously. Lovingly. Because I want to be your bride."

The vast cathedral is filled with sound from the great organ, a long deep bass note that makes the broad stone pillars lining the aisle vibrate, and the tympanum of every ear in the huge celebrity congregation.

Claire Tucker comes forward to where the aisle begins. She is in a floor-length wedding-dress and holds a bouquet of blue and white summer flowers. Other flowers are twined in her hair. Her face is ashine with happiness, but her lips have the subtle smile of a secret knowingness which is seen on Botticelli's *Primavera*.

Jeremy Paxman rises from his pew and takes his place at her side. It is he who will give her away. They advance down the aisle, the ancient limestone paving and memorial slabs now strewn with lilies.

All eyes go back to the man in the ornately-carved and hooded pulpit. But his eyes are on her, his bride-to-be. The organ music soars, a roar of great wings, of pinions beating dark. He

130

stretches his hands towards her. They are drowning in each other's radiant gaze.

"Do you renounce all other men for me?"

And she makes the response: "I do renounce them."

"Am I above all men to you, for ever and ever, world without end?"

And she makes the response: "You are above all men to me. You are the living god to me. For ever and ever, world without end. Amen."

"Amen," he cries.

Tears of joy and deliverance flood the creases of his eyes. He comes swiftly down the turning flight of stairs from the great brass lectern. Cast in the form of a brazen eagle, it is mailed of neck, hooked of bill, fierce of eye; yet it is the eagle of redemption, whose outstretched wingspan forms an angled platform on which rests the great Book in which are inscribed the names, generation unto generation, of the few and the many, the born and the unborn, the mild and the bitter, the quick and the dead. . .

The telephone was ringing again in the hall. Shaken, he stood there transfixed. It rang again, on time, after the expected interval of listening for it to do just that, aghast. It rang again. And again. And again, each time repeating that same double tone followed by the same interval of silence in which the ring still echoed.

He ran out from the kitchen into the hall and stared at the instrument. It rang on and on and on, with an insistent menace of purpose, and for far longer than any caller usually allowed. His mind was seething. It was obvious that *this* caller, too, knew there was someone in the house. Someone who was staring at the telephone at this moment, hearing it ring again and again and again, *watching* it ring, his mind seething, once of the finest of his generation, too shocked and startled and terrified by its insistence and its stridency to answer it. To admit that the person in the house was him.

Then abruptly, with a curious mocking finality, the phone stopped ringing.

Guy Hughes continued to stare at it, waiting for it to ring

again after the usual brief interval. And indeed he seemed to hear the phone ring again once, a tiny fading percussion in his brain or on the memory of his ear, the way yellow leaves a violet after-image, red a green one.

He watched the phone as silence filled the house again. Watched it through that excruciating, longer interval in which a person - certain that someone is at home in the house in which his call has just rung unanswered – wonders if he dialled the correct sequence of digits, and so dials them again.

But the phone did not ring again.

The silence persisted.

Until it became a norm rather than an intense and troubling state of exception.

But it was not a normal silence, the silence of normality. It seemed to be filling the house slowly. Filling it with a curious suave and deadly insistence, like gas. Or the way snow falls overnight from the dark, falls and falls and falls, unceasingly and everywhere, accumulating in drifts and banks, building up in corners and on flat surfaces and on the hooded tops of cars parked in the street and on the streetlights which illuminate the desolation with a deathly orange light.

The house was deaf with silence. But it wasn't the silence of snow. Or the silent whisper of gas. The house was filling with soundlessness itself, like styrofoam granules.

It was trickling in through apertures, a fine, dry, pale, weightless matter building up in each room into a cone whose peak was constantly rising, constantly running away in grains, the way an hourglass empties itself or the desert stops the mouth of a catacomb.

But then, in that denser silence, which Guy Hughes knew with unaccountable certainty to be that of the end, he heard a noise.

Upstairs.

A tiny clatter.

Of something moved

Or lightly rocked.

On a bedside table or dressing-table.
Shocked porcelain figurines
Their grouped silence disturbed.
By a clumsiness.
A hand's
Upstairs
The room
The bedroom
Where his wife
Where Angela
The princess
Asleep
Upstairs
In the bedroom
Her dark thick hair
Her teeth, hardly a filling in them
Though he was not the prince
The bedroom
Where the bed where
Up stairs.

These stairs. A flight. Of thirteen. To the landing. To the door to the bedroom. And the knob to the door.

With a sense of dread he turned the knob counter-clockwise, the familiar loose-spindled quarter-turn, and pushed the door inwards an inch. He stopped for breath. But the door was ajar enough for a hooked paw to widen it and for the cat, long with speed, to slip out past his foot. Guy cried out in shock. The cat fled down the stairs with a swiftness he'd never seen it capable of before.

Guy Hughes turned back to the door. It was cream-painted. In one of the twinned upper panels, at the height of his gaze, a hair from the brush was stuck in the paint like an eyelash. He'd never noticed it before.

But he was here now. It was unavoidable, this room,

inevitable. Like a display in a case, a vacuum sucking him in with the air, though all the rest of the house was filling like a Pharaoh's tomb, dry, pale weightless grains running into the rooms like sand into the whorls and compartments of an empty shell, its accumulating peak constantly rising, constantly running and trickling away in particles.

The door still stood narrowly open.

Pushing at the knob again he stood the door open further on another short arc and went into the room.

He uttered a scream in which disgust and horror vied.

11

Cover Story

After getting back to the office on Monday morning David Fry wasted time in mounting fretfulness and disappointment until eleven, before concluding that Angela Hughes wouldn't be in work again today. Even on flexitime, no one came in later than eleven.

He sat at his desk staring at his screen. Outwardly he was engaged at his job - dealing with warehouse lists, numbers of fan units, code-numbers of different models - but the truth was he was more like a man looking into a flickering fire. Concentration fixed, but elsewhere.

David Fry was gnawed by anxiety.

He'd worked in the office three months now, and the probationary month he and the firm had agreed at the outset was over. Nevertheless he sensed he was still on trial, for various reasons. For his general attitude, which one of the managers had described as "flip". For his off-days - of hangover and general seediness - and his frequent days-off. But also, more worryingly, since more visibly demonstrable, for several acts of negligence or inefficiency which changes of   circumstance or priority had dramatised into costly errors inescapably attributable to himself.

How many more mistakes could he reasonably hope to get away with by claiming unfamiliarity with specific office practice or blaming a computer system failure (as with his deleting of a vital file)? Not too fucking many, he felt.

And now he'd lost or mislaid another document entrusted to him for processing. A real document, this time, a signed hard-copy-original, a three-page contractual specification he couldn't find. He'd only discovered the loss late on Thursday afternoon, after Angela Hughes had apparently already left the office.

David Fry wasn't concerned at first. The document wouldn't be needed till the following week, Tuesday or Wednesday at the earliest, and he knew he couldn't have deleted this one since it wasn't on his computer. It hadn't been binned, burnt, shredded or deep-sixed either, not by him anyway. So at least it still existed somewhere, instead of in the sky-ether of entropy or wherever it was where erased files and unreceived emails went to die. Also, Angela Hughes had been incidentally involved with this item of paperwork, had offered instructions on how to deal with it, and he'd conceived an initially indolent optimism that she may have filed it somewhere on his behalf or by mistake, if tidiness or efficiency could be called a mistake. She was always telling him to keep his desktop clean, by which she mean both the physical litter on his office desk and the icons and folders cluttering his computer screen.

He'd therefore simply assumed that Angela Hughes would be in work as usual the following day - the Friday - and postponed any pressing concern about the missing papers till then. He'd got used to relying on Angela's experience and help in an exploitative relationship of hapless tyro and brisk office pedant which she seem to find mildly rewarding.

David Fry, naturally, didn't feel himself to be one of those who are intended for office work. In fact he detested it, and several of his current colleagues. But it was a paying job, and his girlfriend had just told him there was a baby on the way, which she assured him was his.

The secret no one else took account of — he'd never told anyone, not even his girlfriend - was that David Fry wanted to be a writer, and dealing with warehouse storage inventories or orders for Swedish-made ventilation units designed for factories and offices didn't even seem to him to offer bankable experience. Just tedium on an light-industrial scale at a little above the average wage. Once the baby was born, he intended to take the maximum allowable period of paternity leave and start writing a novel. He had no compulsive idea for a subject yet, though it had always seemed to him that his own life possessed a fascination granted to the lives of few others. But he was sure that as soon as there was a baby in the house – or the flat he supposed he and his girlfriend would have to find - he would have contrived, for the first time, the necessary interregnum of salaried leisure in which to float a new career.

But being able to claim this term of paternity leave was conditional on his staying in his job until the birth. A condition which might come into question if the missing contract remained unfound – as it still was when he went home on at five o'clock on Friday afternoon, despite his having spent a good deal of that day unobtrusively searching for it in likely places, including Angela Hughes's filing trays and desk-drawers.

So, when not drinking and clubbing, fishing for dace or watching Test cricket from Australia by satellite into the small hours, David Fry had spent a sporadically worried weekend. His mood was not lightened by the failure to contact Angela Hughes by phone at home, and by the obstructive behaviour of her husband, who seemed to resent her being bothered by office matters out of office hours. He'd spoken to the geezer previously when he'd tried telephoning his wife in work, of course; so he'd heard David's voice before. But to be identified so instantly had seemed uncanny. Clair fucking voyant almost.

Then, when Angela had failed to come to the office on Monday morning too, David Fry's anxiety had risen again, like a fever reading. After some thought, or rather a blank period of staring at his screen in further irresolution, he'd again tried phoning her at home, hoping that her husband would himself be back at *his* job after the weekend and that even if Angela were too unwell to come in to work, he, David, would be able to talk to her and get clarification on where the lost document might be (or, at worst, advice on how to conceal or mitigate its loss).

But though he'd tried her number several times during Monday – and let the phone ring for a long time, a signal of his own hectoring sense of urgency and on the recognition that she might be ill upstairs in bed, and the phone downstairs in the hallway, and it would take her time to reach it - there was no answer.

It merely rang. And rang. And rang. And rang. And rang. And rang. Until he came to sense a futile tone to its ringing, that of a phone ringing unheard in an empty house.

On top of all this, he felt bloody lousy. He'd been incubating a heavy cold over the weekend, and by Monday it was at its vilest stage, every breath bubbling with snot. He'd used up two packets of tissues by lunchtime and spent the rest of the day trudging to the gents' toilets to evacuate his sore nostrils into squares of paper towelling pulled from the dispenser beside the washbasin, each time inspecting the result distastefully before crumpling and flushing the little weighted shuttlecock down the lavatory. His mucus was now the colour and consistency of unripe rhubarb, stewed.

If he hadn't felt in an uncertain, even threatened position – and if he hadn't taken the bloody Tuesday off the week before - he'd have complained of feeling ill and gone home. But, now he was in, he thought he'd better stick it out. The neon strip lighting in the office seemed increasingly strange to his eyes. It emitted a buzz he'd never noticed before. He spent a miserable afternoon looking at figures on his screen and going in and out of the toilets to blow his nose. The neon light in the toilets was louder, pitched almost at a whine. But he felt an odd sense of sanctuary in the calm and solitude and the noise of trickling water, and each time he went back to his desk with reluctance. Out in the office people addressed occasional remarks or questions to him, and he had to keep making answers, though he didn't wish to talk. His own voice sounded unreal in his head, and he was developing a sore throat too.

By four o'clock it was painful to swallow his spit. He thought about going out to the newsagents' shop across the street and buying some sweets to suck. But he remembered he might still have the remains of a packet in his briefcase, a little tight-wrapped cube of two or three blackcurrant-flavour Tunes.

As he found the sweets some papers slid from a brochure he'd taken out while looking for them. It was the lost contract. He recognised it instantly. Three printed pages stapled together in the top left-hand corner. It had somehow slipped in between pages of a magazine advertising autumn-break holidays in Turkey, which he'd picked up in a travel agents' shop the other day. He'd kept this not because he wished to visit Turkish resorts on a package tour but because the way the slim, wet-haired girl in the lime-green bikini on the cover smiled, and the way the water beaded on her brown skin, caught at his heart.

David Fry had known his girlfriend for some time, and they'd early on got into the habit of going to bed together when they were both boozed up; and it was a hard habit to break, even though his girlfriend was not really very pretty and he could foresee his mother thinking her common. But now the situation, which had seemed as casual and fluid as their pubbing and clubbing habits, had crystallised, like ice-cubes hardening in the tray. His girlfriend had told him she was pregnant, that he was the father of this baby - if that was the term for the tiny, mouselike embryo she was now carrying - and soon, he supposed, they would get married. He had accepted all this. But it still seemed to him a fictional situation, and one of hackneyed banality.

Nevertheless, when he thought about it, and what it would be like to be a father, and husband to this wife, the future stirred his heart with fear.

Which was why he'd been touched by the girl on the cover of the travel brochure. It wasn't even lust he'd felt for her. It was more a poignant and sentimental grief akin to a sense of primal loss.

It was emotional, as if for a real person, someone he knew, though he'd never even seen her photograph before. She was just an anonymous model who was trying to make a living by wearing scanty beachwear or knotted kangas (as she did inside the brochure, head on one side, smiling); and by making sure she always had clean hair and clear eyes and white teeth, and stayed thin and brown.

This aside, he didn't know a single fact about her.

But he did know she must have a boyfriend somewhere, a

lover, who had a great deal to be joyful for; and that it wasn't him; and that this was one of those universal personal tragedies which are the reverse of those in the Hokkaido-Nansei-Oki tsunami or the Turkish earthquake in that they're not increased but diminished by numbering so many victims.

12

Number 31

To languish in uncertainty was one thing. But to anguish in it was another. It was the difference between a passive vegetative condition and a state of active worry. Hyperactive, even.

And Terry Goss's problem was he was a worrier.

All weekend he had anguished at his lover's silence, now of three days' duration. Anguished at it in the obsessive, pessimistic way only a marital loser, a forty-three year-old divorcee and chronic celibate, can anguish; an adult single who's learned to dread the loveless urban weekend even more than as an adolescent he'd feared the wan, suburban Sunday, its hormonal loneliness.

And in middle age the torments of aroused lubricity were worse.

The truth was, Terry Goss had started nursing unexpected hopes of a future conjugal happiness, with what he thought of as unlimited amatory access and mutual delight. In the present he enjoyed an adulterous partner already willing (at least, until Thursday last) to cooperate in liberating his long-contained desire - so brief its spasms, so momentous yet so frugal, hardly a teaspoonful each time, yet the lubricant that oiled the axle of the universe! Who'd even take him in the mouth sometimes with lavish spontaneity.

Who met him weekly or fortnightly for this.

And who sent him chatty or jokey or sometimes risqué text messages daily, from work, from her car, even from her bathroom at home, under cover of her own flush-water.

But now these had stopped.

All weekend he waited for his mobile phone to buzz and slide, buzz and slide on his desk-top. He was disappointed not to have heard from her on Friday. By the end of Saturday this had worsened into anxiety; and by Sunday evening it was a crisis. Was something wrong? Was she punishing him for something? Had she changed her mind about their relationship?

His mind swarmed like an unhappy anthill.

By Monday morning he had achieved, at intervals, a bleak-eyed calm. As he drove to work it was a sunny morning, a light touched with the desperate mortality of all things. He had a meeting with the Administrative Officer scheduled for 9 o'clock on Monday morning, but as soon as that was over (it was nearly 9.45), he closed the door of his office and rang Angela Hughes's office number. He was told she hadn't arrived for work yet.

He put the phone down and wondered what to do now.

The phone fucked up your life, he realised. And spoiled your day too, at the very least. Since he'd become Dean and, shortly afterwards, started seeing Angela, things had got worse. You spent hour after hour with it clutched in one hand and a pen in the other, taking notes and pumping or earholing people you didn't especially want to talk to, but who were always in, always there when you called, always available. Whereas the one person you longed to talk to you couldn't talk to, not on the weekend anyway. You could only do so furtively on working days and in working hours and on certain numbers, and then only briefly.

It was another of the killing stress conditions of modern life, he meditated. Email, the internet, the mobile phone, all these instantaneous connections, and the daily or even minute-by-minute contact they encouraged, were part of the same constant condition, which was one of induced emergency. So that when you couldn't reach someone for a couple of hours or on a particular day – let alone over a whole weekend - it became an information crisis. Or a neurosis. (Why weren't they answering? Why were they ignoring you?) How had people managed in the old days, with letters sent and brought by mule and pack-horse, by sailboat and train?

Terry Goss sat musing on the desperate emotional

insecurities of lovers separated by war, revolution or famine, and lacking news or even any likelihood of news. How did they cope with the months and years of waiting? – of inbuilt delay? Where did they find such stolidity, such stoicism? *He* was frazzled, worn threadbare, after a few days of unanswered SMSes . .

He was deliberating whether to ring Angela at home when his secretary knocked, came in and informed him that Guy Hughes hadn't shown up to teach his 9.15 class; the seminar room it was to take place in was still locked and the students were congregated around the coffee machine.

"What? Again? Has he phoned in sick?"

No, he hadn't.

"Can you believe it?" Terry said.

Himself unable to, he sat there. The secretary waited with a sympathetic expression.

"He comes in late Friday, then takes the afternoon off with a hangover! Now he's stretching it to Monday morning too!"

Terry laughed inanely.

"Of course it could be a new hangover."

He picked up the phone.

"Alright," he told his secretary. "I'll deal with it."

He watched her leave.

He looked at the phone. Though infuriated by Guy Hughes's insolently casual attitude towards his teaching responsibilities – and at having to find replacement lecturers for his classes at short notice - Terry had also found a pretext to dial Angela's home number: a sequence of digits he'd written in his address book, and knew by heart, but never used. He'd always contacted her on her office phone or, more usually, her mobile. But this morning she wasn't in her office. And there was still this problem with her mobile. (He assumed and hoped it was a problem with her mobile.) His mobile had had told him that his first few messages had been delivered, had reached hers. Despite their mounting urgency, however, she hadn't answered them. Then other messages had not even been delivered, were still circling in some electronic limbo. (A phone problem seemed the only acceptable excuse. Unless she really did suffer from migraines, as Guy had claimed.)

He still couldn't ring Angela openly, not if Guy was at home, which (since he wasn't at work) he might be. (Though he might also show up in college late again at any moment, pleading another problem with his car.)

His mind gnawed at a variety of possibilities and uncertainties.

But he, Terry, wasn't only Angela's lover. He was Guy's boss. If he rang that number, and Guy answered, he could ask why he hadn't come in, why he hadn't rung in to explain his absence, and why the fuck his students were left hanging around the cafeteria again, as if that was the sole purpose of the call. On the other hand, if Guy had left for work, and Angela answered, they could talk at last.

He was still staring at the phone. He put it down. Then he willed himself to pick it up again. But he couldn't key the number.

He had an ominous feeling. A whole weekend without a text message and the fact that neither Guy nor Angela was in work that Monday morning could only indicate a crisis in the household. And the only crisis he could envisage was that his affair with Angela had been discovered.

He couldn't face the chance of having Guy answer the phone knowing that.

On the other hand, one way or the other, he, Terry, had to know if he knew.

He felt faintly sick with the dilemma of inaction he'd caused himself.

Finally, he went out, gave his secretary the number and asked her to ring the house instead. On a precautionary instinct he left her office and went back into his own. He closed the door. He looked at the big teaching timetable and wondered about arranging cover for Guy's classes for the rest of the day. Then he stared out of the window tensely. He wandered out a few minutes later.

"Any luck with that phone call?"

The secretary shook her head.

"No answer."

Terry Goss rolled his eyes to the ceiling at the fecklessness of his colleague, an expression of martyrdom which recalled the swooning gaze of saints and Christs in depictions of religious passion. This response was exaggerated by partial relief that at least a denunciatory monologue concerning his adultery with Guy's wife had not been triggered by the call.

"You didn't manage to talk to his wife?" he elaborated pointlessly.

"There was no answer at all."

"Maybe I should give her a bell at work,"

Terry Goss proposed this for no reason except that circumstance made it possible for him to make further mention of the woman he'd been conducting an affair with for the last six months, even enabling him to imply an intimacy that extended to knowing her office telephone number. It was a loosely-coded boast. This infraction of a habitual secrecy should have afforded him a furtive pleasure. But today it only voiced a despair of indecision, since in reality he'd already rung her at work and learnt she wasn't there.

He waited until eleven before phoning her office again. This time, when told she still hadn't arrived, he asked:

"Is she off sick?"

The secretary the telephonist had put him through to was the same woman who'd been asked to call Angela Hughes at home to enquire as to her absence.

"Actually, we're not sure. She hasn't rung in sick. Or to say she'll be in late today. And she doesn't seem to be answering the phone at home."

"Oh," Terry Goss said.

He stood there for a moment, clutching the phone. He was trying to think how to elicit more information.

"Will that be all?" the secretary asked. She had a caller on another line.

"Yes. Thank you."

Terry Goss put the phone down.

He had other calls to make too. A whole list of them. But that was work. College administration. This was emotion. And in his emotional life, aside from Angela, for the last six months he'd had no one else to call, and no one who called him. Since their fortuitous meeting in a Sainsbury's car-park, the first time they'd spoken to each other outside the college's social calendar, Angela Hughes had filled his life, tremulously but to the brim – filled it too, it should be said, with the misery of missing her, with the desperation of wanting her, of not being with her. With evenings and weekends of a solitary bachelorhood which seemed even unhappier, or more pointedly unhappy, than they had been before. But at least now it was an unhappiness haunted by absence and desire, by the tension of love and lust, an ache which was a greater plenitude of being than any he'd experienced since his youth.

It was true: this unexceptional forty-seven year-old woman, had made Terry Goss feel like a love-struck teenager. The caution and mutual tentativeness of their first meetings even recalled his early shynesses with girls and theirs with him, as if adultery itself were a discovery not of middleaged pragmatism but a new, radically more innocent adolescence.

Nothing changed, he'd realised. You got older. Greyer. Heavier. But you never grew up. Even at forty-three, the human heart bruised easier than a peach.

And it was wonderful.

All that working Monday, and all Monday night at home, Terry Goss endured another stint of agonised irresolution. He rang Angela's office again in the afternoon, and they'd still heard nothing from her. He continued to ring the Hughes's home number on an irregular, impromptu basis, as if on the off-chance of surprising someone who was passing the phone into answering on a reflex. But no one did.

He slept badly again, and suffered dreams perfused with a brooding sense of darkness and confinement, of being trapped in a red Royal Mail pillar-box and having to maintain a crippling permanent crouch to peer out of the hooded slit opposite his eyes, as from the visor of some great iron helmet.

When he woke he felt unrested, and was filled with fear, as if he was going into hospital that day for an operation. But his mind was made up.

He left the house early and drove the route he'd taken so often to his rendez-vous with Angela, when she'd left her car in the car-park at the leisure centre and he'd driven her back to his house in his. (She didn't like to drive directly there in her car. In case, she said, her husband checked the mileage.) This time, though, it was to her house that he drove. Her and Guy's.

He knew the number, but he'd never been to the house before. He had to drive past it as there was no possibility of parking outside.

It was the usual suburban street. Semi-detached houses, cars tight-parked at either kerb and a lane in the middle for moving cars to cruise from one junction to the next in search of a space. He had to turn the corner into the next street until he saw a car pulling out of a space he could back his into.

He walked back to the house, went up the short path, rang the doorbell. That 31 was a prime number struck him. Was that a good omen? His own age, 43, and Angela's, 47 were prime numbers too, though of course that wouldn't always be the case. On the other hand, all of her phone numbers, and his, were divisible. . . He knew all this was nonsense. Superstition. But he'd lived for some time in thrall to the psychopathology of numerals in his daily life.

He stood waiting, looking at the two digits, of moulded white plastic, serifed, each held to the door by a single galvanised screw with a Philips head. Although he knew the phone had been ringing in the house with futile and regular persistence all the previous day and much of last night, this morning he was nervously expecting the doorbell to be answered and the door abruptly opened. He wore a bright, concerned expression on his face, and was braced to encounter either Guy or Angela. He was there as Guy's colleague and superior, and had resolved on a brisk style and form of greeting serviceable for either spouse, in the likelihood that the other was inside the house too, and in hearing distance.

But neither appeared. Nor did ringing the doorbell with a longer, more urgent pressure of his thumb result in any sign that either would.

He bent to lift the hinged flap of the letter-box, and looked into the hall.

He called: "Guy!"

Then, with a thrill of illicitness at using her first name: "Angela!"

He stayed there, peering into the hallway through the slit, an uncomfortable posture which he maintained long enough to understand the meaning of his troubled dream the night before.

The light was poor, and he could make out very little in the closed and unlit hallway. Stairs. A dresser. Doors, off. Yet he kept peering in, as if in expectancy of a sign, clue, revelation, a dark familiar shape flitting on tiptoe from one doorway to another. He was still troubled by the possibility that Guy Hughes had discovered his affair with Angela. Yet if he and Guy were going to have to have a showdown it would, he knew, at least be better to precipitate it here, in Guy's own house, than risk an impromptu shouting-match next time they ran into each other in a corridor in college. . .

He watched and listened. He wondered if the couple were listening too, crouched inside, in silence in one of the closed rooms, locked in some climacteric state of emotional siege, not answering the doorbell, not picking up the phone, not even calling in to their respective jobs to say they were taking the day off.

It even struck him that Guy might be holding her as a marital hostage, refusing to let her call her lover, or even leave the house, and Terry Goss had a tormenting vision of her in a room, gagged, wrists bound behind her back, breasts thrust forward in that way women did on the covers of paperback thrillers circa 1950, proud and sweetly unwilling victims. . .

His eyesight must have adjusted to the gloom in the hall, because after crouching at the letter-box for a little longer he discerned a long dark shape at the foot of the far wall. Was it a garment of some kind? A pullover perhaps, simply dropped or even flung there? Whatever it was, it lay along the skirting-board: an unlikely place for a garment, even a cast-off one – or for anything else. There were what looked like two hooked appendages sticking up out of it.

He kept peering in at it.

It seemed, finally, less through an act of perception than an effort of imaginative construction – as in those *trompe-l'oeil* psychological tests where either a candlestick or the profiles of two human faces may be identified – that he realised the garment was in fact a cat, that it lay at full length on its back, and that its front legs were sticking up in the air.

In the same instant of accepting the fact that the cat was dead, he comprehended the stain of blood, a smeared rose that bloomed on a dark stem on the white wall above the body. It must have been hurled or swung against the wall with astonishing violence.

Now he knew there was something desperately wrong in the house. But it still made no sense. An intruder might kill a dog guarding the property or which would alert the occupants.

But a cat?

Thoughts of dark rites troubled Terry Goss's mind. He straightened, and let go of the flap of the letter-box. It snapped shut on its sprung hinge.

He went in turn to the two houses next to the Hughes's. He rang the doorbell at the first, number 29 (yet another prime number) and rapped the knocker of the other, 33 (a product of 3 and 11), there being no bell. But there was no answer at either house.

He looked at his watch. It was 9.35: past the hour when people left for work. And past the time when he should be heading for college too.

He stood on the pavement outside the Hughes's house, irresolute.

It was only now he noticed that Angela's red Vectra was one of those cars parked along the gutter. Then that Guy's metallic-blue Peugeot 307 was parked next-but-one along (he and Guy often parked in the same street behind the college, and he recognised the car).

Somewhere in another street a car alarm went off. He stood listening to it, but no longer irresolute, as if the noise had jarred him to a decision.

13

A Routine Emergency

The police patrol car had been only a few streets away, having driven there very fast through rush-hour traffic for a reported car break-in. A woman watching from her window had seen two youths walking along the pavement close to the line of cars parked along the kerb and glancing into them. One of the youths had brought out a hammer from under his coat and with two rapid blows, savage in their determination, smashed in the rear window of one of the cars, a silver Audi, setting off its alarm. He'd reached in to unlock the door, withdrawn his arm, jerked the door open. He'd taken a black briefcase from the back seat. Shoving it under one arm, he and his companion had run off to the end of the street, where a car had pulled up for them to get in and then driven off. The woman had rung the police. When the patrol car arrived the car's rear door was agape onto the pavement and its alarm still sounding.

As the younger of the two policemen was establishing the facts of this incident, another emergency report came in. This one sounded even more routine. Receiving the outline details in the patrol car, the senior officer presumed it to be another instance of a busybody neighbour – though in this case reporting apparently suspicious events for which there was probably a simple and entirely lawful reason. The account involved a cat and an unanswered phone. When didn't it? Invariably it turned out that someone had gone into hospital or left on holiday without telling the people next door.

When they'd found the street and arrived outside number

31 the patrol car had to be left double-parked, the blue light turning slowly on the top, as there wasn't a free space along either kerb. The witness who'd reported the incident was waiting for them, wheeling up and down along the pavement in a ghost dance of anxiety and impatience while talking urgently into his mobile phone. But he terminated his call promptly and, when asked, confirmed he was Mr. Goss, Dr. Goss actually, and it was he who had rung the police.

"Are you a doctor, sir?" the younger officer asked.

"Not that kind of a doctor," Terry Goss said. "Not a medical doctor."

"So what kind of a doctor are you, sir?"

"A Doctor of Philosophy."

"Philosophy," the young officer repeated.

"I'm a teacher," Terry Goss explained. "Or rather, er, Dean of Studies. I work in the Art College. I have a PhD."

Terry Goss perceived anew, from the young policeman's expression, what he had already learned in bitterness many times. That people seemed for some reason contemptuous of his status rather than impressed by it. But it was a lesson he could never believe in enough to withhold the information.

All this took place on the pavement, while Sergeant Stiles stayed in the car to finish writing notes for his report on the previous incident to which they'd been called. He ceased his jottings to listen as the witness began to recount to Constable Andrews the circumstances preceding his phone call to the emergency services. The witness then led Andrews to the front door of number 31.

Terry Goss stooped, peered in through the letter-box, as if to vet that all was still properly in place. He straightened, stepped back and invited the young constable to do the same with a directorial gesture, triggering pedagogic memories of getting film students to look at a set through the lens of a mounted film-camera.

The policeman stared at him as if conscious of this act of patronage. He squatted to stare in through the letter-box.

"Light's not that brilliant," he said. "I can't see a bloody

152

thing."

"You have to wait till your eyes adjust," Terry Goss said.

The policeman showed by a further glance of disparagement that he had a better idea. He went back to the car and returned with a large black Maglite. Then he squatted beside it and shone it through the slit.

He stayed there for a while, playing the torch's light in, eyelids shifting as took in details of the interior.

"Jesus," he said.

He straightened up and looked at Terry Goss. Then he went back to the car, went around it to the far window and, squatting down in the road, jouncing lightly on his hams, spoke quietly and rapidly to the suddenly keener face of his seated colleague. Then he straightened, brushing the creases out of the back of his trousers, and stood back for the other man to open the car door and get out.

When they reached the front door Andrews handed Stiles the torch. Terry Goss noticed that, like himself, the older policeman was too stiff of limb to squat, but crouched uncomfortably to peer in at the letter-box.

Then he too stood back from the door. He looked at his colleague, then signalled towards their car with a slight jerk of his head.

"Perhaps you'll excuse us for a moment," he said to Terry Goss, and they left him waiting in the porch of number 31.

Eventually he wandered out onto the pavement again. The two policemen were standing in low-volume discussion beside their car. He offered a comment but it was ignored while Sergeant Stiles, in the unwelcome presence of a member of the public, opened the car door and got into the driving seat again to call in a preliminary report or for instructions. He pressed a button and the lowered window went up between himself and the over-eager bystander. They were all like that. They all thought they were star witnesses. Terry Goss nodded helpfully at the rebuff, wandered a few tactful yards further off, and paced as if plunged in thought. The other policeman was ringing the doorbell at Number 29.

"There's no one in," Terry Goss called out. "I tried both sides."

The policeman did not acknowledge this information. He rang the bell again anyway and waited, looking up at the front of the house shrewdly as if idly assessing the chances of scaling it. Terry Goss was left to look on, and weigh the full weight of his own superfluity. Then his mobile phone rang. Earlier, after phoning for the police, he'd rung in to tell his secretary he'd be in late today. There were some administrative matters he asked to be attended to, but had cut short his instructions when the police arrived. Now there was further query about the details. He could have dealt with all this later. Or he could go back now to where he'd parked and look for the papers in his briefcase, which would at least give him something to do. To be seen to be doing.

The senior policeman was still giving or receiving instructions in the patrol car. Terry Goss attracted his attention through the closed window. He showed his phone, then pointed in the direction of the street junction and went through a dumbshow of walking fingers and facial mime. He tapped his watch and showed a palm and five fingers to indicate how long he'd be gone. In the closed car the policeman, listening and speaking, nodded and looked up at him without altruism.

As Terry walked back towards his car the other policeman was going to scout around the back of the semi-detached pair of houses and another sky-blue and white police patrol car was arriving in the street.

Terry Goss made the call brief. Just before he concluded it his secretary added that there had still been no word from Guy Hughes or any sign that he'd be in that day either.

"No," Terry Goss said.

He hesitated as to whether he should tell her anything. It was a choice between garrulousness or laconicism.

"I wouldn't hold my breath till you see him," he said finally. "Not if I was you." Then he added: "I'm not sure when I'll be in either."

As he turned the corner on his way back to number 31 the

second patrol car was driving off. Terry Goss arrived in time to find the younger policeman carrying a red steel post with an attitude of expectancy. It had a handle welded at one end, D-shaped like a spade's but slightly canted. Another handle was positioned like the dorsal fin on a fish or a vane on a small rocket.

As he lugged it to the door of No. 31 it was clear from his briskly possessive air that no one was going to deprive Andrews of the chance to use it. He set himself at a stance and, gripping tighter, heaved it back then forward: a concise, vehement arc. The blow landed with a splintering noise at the side of the front door, just under the lock-plate. The door swung open inwards. He stood looking at it, as if he'd always wanted to do that.

"Just stand back, please," the other officer told Terry Goss.

The younger policeman laid the steel ram in the porch, attentive of the green glazed decorative tiling. He stood and exchanged a glance with his colleague, as the two prepared to enter. Terry Goss understood that glance later. It was a look that was instinctive between men who'd learnt never to be sure of what they may be walking in to find.

Both policemen went into the hallway, the older man ahead and carrying the torch. But he put the light on as soon as he saw the switch. Terry Goss waited before following them in. Through all that ensued he expected at any moment to be instructed to wait outside. But perhaps the policemen were concentrating too anxiously on what they might find.

The cat lay like an old fur mitten at the base of the wall. It was lying on its back and looked curled and dried-up, as if it had shrunk into death. The bloodstain on the wall where it had been brained had darkened and dried too, though profuse enough when fresh to have run in a droplet as far as the skirting board, then down over its mouldings.

Constable Andrews wrinkled his nose at the small body in fascinated disgust.

But there was more to come.

All the downstairs doors were closed. But Sergeant Stiles

barely glanced at them. Impelled by the certainty of experience he looked up the stairs, an alert profile. He started to mount the treads. The other policeman followed, then Terry Goss, loiteringly, at an ambiguous onlooker's distance.

One by one they filed first into the room to which the door stood already ajar. Then halted inside, now grouping instinctively to a threesome. Hands over their mouths and noses, they stood staring at the body in the bed.

Only Terry Goss knew it was Angela Hughes, and even he couldn't be sure at first.

"Oh God, no," he said.

One side of her face lay open. Part had been eaten away.

The three men reeled out of the room at the same moment, gasping for cleaner air, almost squeezing together in the doorway.

They stood on the landing looking at each other and then not looking at each other.

"Jesus Christ," Andrews said. He was distressed.

Stiles was stooped, hands on knees, as if after a race.

"Did you recognise that person, sir?" he asked after a short while.

"Yes," Terry Goss said. "It's Mrs. Hughes."

His voice faltered on the lie of calling her that. But even now he had the adulterer's alibi of formal relations to maintain.

After a short period recovering the rhythm of their breath, like people at the top of a steep slope, the two policemen went into the other upstairs rooms, looking into each hastily for corroboration of its emptiness, and closing the door again in relief. Terry Goss went downstairs, clasping his head.

He was standing in the hallway when the policemen rejoined him.

Andrews looked back up the stairs. His face was pursed in disgust or disbelief.

"I can't get over that," he said.

He meant that he found what he'd seen incredible rather than insurmountable. He shook his head.

"All her face. . ."

He looked at the two other men in turn.

"Why would it do that?"

Sergeant Stiles looked back up the stairs. He was swarthy and had amber eyes. He'd taken off his peaked cap and his hair was grey and bristle-close, but the specks of stubble in his shaved cheeks were black as filings. A odour of brilliantine came from the cap's sweated lining.

"It must have been shut in there with her. What's it going to live on up there? Flower water? Air?"

Terry Goss moaned and covered his eyes with his hands and drew them down his cheeks, showing the pink of his underlids.

"The next question is," said Stiles, "who did that to the cat?"

He thought about laying his cap on the hall table, lining uppermost, and almost did so. Then he remembered this was a crime scene and put it back on instead, and set it straight.

One still following the other, and one by one, the officers visited the ground-floor rooms. All were empty, at least of anything gruesome: just unoccupied rooms in a suburban home. The two men were encouraged to the hope that they'd found all there was to find. The absent Mr. Hughes had assumed a sullen-faced Identikit clarity, that of a confirmed murder suspect and fugitive.

They joined Terry Goss in the hall a second time. Their preliminary investigation of the house, and the scene of a death, was complete. Time, surely – opportunity, anyway - to leave the building, go to the patrol car, call in and report what they'd found. Time to stretch the striped plastic tape everywhere like bunting, and then wait in the street, in the fresh air, having done what was needed to isolate the murder-room like a set in a stage whodunit, leaving it for the pathologist and the crime-site specialists, the men in paper suits and surgical masks. The boys who'd seen it all and placed it in a ziplock bag or dug it up as bones or carried it out on a stretcher underneath a sheet, and didn't scare.

It was Sergeant Stiles who decided to explore the small garden behind the house too: the nag of professional thoroughness on his part, or an unfinished sense of the inevitability and dread that now hung over the three of them.

"Better just have a shifty out the back," he said. "In case."

And so it was he who then led them into the garage.

The body hung by a short rope from a hook in a beam. A low stool lay on its side on the concrete floor, but too obviously somehow, as if not really toppled but placed at that angle for illustrative purposes.

"Oh Jesus," the young policeman said again. "Oh Jesus fucking Christ."

Terry Goss stood staring. Then stared somewhere else. He'd realised that what he'd thought was a plum forced into the mouth in some grotesque mockery was only a black protruding tongue

Then the other policeman was asking him, "And this is Mr Hughes, is it, sir?"

He couldn't look at the face again.

But he said: "Yes."

He couldn't even look at the feet. Only inches separated the dead man's heels and toes from the concrete floor they must have dangled or kicked above.

After a while he found himself gazing at the three painted canvases instead. They were, it struck him, positioned like that as if to be noticed. To be seen in the order of noticed events. Like a suicide note propped on a mantlepiece. One painting stood on the easel, and the other two, smaller ones on the floor, were leaned against its front legs, in triangular arrangement.

It resembled a triple crucifixion scene, in vaguely Pop-art style. The figures to the right and left were not of two thieves but the voluptuous and near-naked bodies of women each bound by ropes to a cross splayed like an X. One of the faces was blindfold, the other gagged or muzzled. The figure in the central canvas was not crucified, but hung slumped like a long bag at the end of another rope. One hand gripped the phallus, erect above stubbled testicles, like a plucked turkey held up by the neck.

Looking closer, he saw that the head above the clenched

fist *was* a plucked turkey's. Its eye was glazed over and the red beak parted in a final squawk.

There was some lettering in white on the larger central panel of the triptych:

At the top it said:

"The Last Coming."

And across the bottom of the canvas:

"Ejaculation: the hanged man's last request."

There were other paintings too, he saw. A great many of them. They stood at the foot of the walls or against objects in the garage, on show like paintings exhibited for sale in the street, a row propped along the railings. Like the three canvases he'd noticed first – and which he could tell from the glisten of the paint had probably been painted last – they were very directly, even crudely painted, like obscene mural drawings in a public toilet. The fact that they were largely in umbers and ochre-colours reinforced this, as if they'd been scrawled in excrement.

14

A Never-Ending Story

It took a long time for Terry Goss to recover from the loss of Angela Hughes. And he was never to cease his sorrowful inward lamentation of theirs as the great, the tragically unaccomplished passion of his life – in a life that, like most lives, from the usual adolescent crushes on, was prolific in unaccomplished passions. Yet she outranked all the others, not only in that a relationship had actually existed – had been consummated, time and time again, in heat and squalor, guilt and joy - but because she was perfected in death: she had become, or was presumed by him to be, a victim of her love for him. In addition, her death had bequeathed to the surviving partner of the relationship that deep, unspoken, unspeakable consolation that at least she wasn't sleeping with anybody else. Terry Goss was never to know that it was not the discovery of his adulterous affair with Angela Hughes, the wife of a colleague, which had precipitated the double tragedy at number 31.

It took a long time, too, for the flashbacks, that persistent cliché of film narrative, to cease. The thought of the famished cat, shut in with a corpse, then slammed by the tail against the wall in grief or rage by the murderer, was a memory that in time faded to circumstantiality. To an old grey long fur glove stretched along a skirting-board. But he never would quite annul the recurrent vision of what had the cat had done. He kept seeing the woman he had loved with half her face gnawed, on a soiled bed in a strange bedroom lined with her trinkets.

The most searing of these involuntary rewitnessings, though, was of her husband hanged by his own hand in his own garage. The bulged-out blue stare and black tongue. The dangled body brought its own tacit narrative, too: part of what film-makers termed the back-story. The small, quick, pragmatic preparations for such a death, the necessary shortening of the rope, which had trailed so much slack from that low beam. And the delicacy – or inexactitude – of judgement which had kept both feet only a fraction clear of the concrete floor. Terry Goss never ceased being able to imagine an involuntary change of mind in the victim, the reaching, not-quite-skittering toecaps, the twisting, lurching burden: the brief desperate last dance. Then immense inertness, as the weight of the body passed up out of itself into the stiffness of the rope.

But forgetting all this might have been hard too for the two police officers, men who, he supposed, went on some daily or weekly or monthly basis into rooms or buildings where an atrocity or catastrophe had occurred, and had to confront it each time with calm and practicality, then be ready to go on again, to cope with the next. The next incident among all those hideous incidents you read about in newspaper headlines or glimpsed on the tv news, and looked away from even then. The found bodies of abducted and many-times dishonoured children left to starve to death in a cage in a cellar. Those of other children cut dead from the wreckage of the coach that was taking them on a school trip.

He declined the police suggestion that he talk to a counsellor, though he did submit to an interview arranged for him with a gross earnest woman who repeatedly termed herself "a social-work professional". He came out of the room meditating without compunction or ingratitude an indomitable detestation of her and all her kind. In any case, he'd never mentioned to the police his love affair with Angela, and he couldn't trust the confidentiality of anyone they might recommend.

But a few weeks after the events of that Monday he went to see his former wife. He felt obscurely that it was either this or a priest, and he wasn't a Catholic, even though as it happened he was reading Graham Greene at that time: *The End Of The Affair*.

He wasn't anything. Once, for a joke, when filling in a

form, under *Religion* he'd written "Sun Worshipper". But he wasn't even that. He burnt raw on a beach, like an albino. He was Dean of Fine Arts, he was forty-three years old, and he was tragically alone. (Was 1 a prime number? Or the prime of all numbers?)

He sat opposite Barbara in the small kitchen of her flat, which he'd never entered before, and told her everything that had happened, at least so far as he understood it.

She sat patiently and attentively in the other chair and listened, only occasionally asking a question or interjecting. Purely as gossip – as uncut melodrama - the story held its drama and fascination right to the end, and then throughout a lengthy inquest of discussion.

They fell silent. Eventually Terry asked after their daughter, who was at university in York. He received the vague answer usual among parents who have no idea what their children do in their daily or nightly lives but that they are at least continuing to maintain the front of a degree course.

They were silent again.

"They never had children?" Barbara asked.

The Hugheses she meant, he knew.

"No," he said. "Don't ask me why not."

He hesitated. It struck him that he could well be the greatest living authority on the Hughes's marriage. He should say something over it. He gestured, as at something self-evident.

"Well, for years he didn't have a full-time lectureship. They were living in flats and so on. Then I think she got a decent job, and he finally got made up to Senior Lecturer. So then they bought that house. And they both had to keep working to pay it off. Probably a biggish mortgage. I think they, you know, joined the property market late, and when prices were high."

The truth was that Terry Goss had no idea why they hadn't had children. He had never asked.

But Barbara nodded to say it all made sense. During all this time, several hours, in which Terry had finished the bottle of wine she'd opened, she found that he no longer bored and irritated her – though when he'd rung and asked to come over, she had

162

regretted agreeing almost as soon as she'd done so.

Only the week before she'd terminated a relationship with another divorced man, whom she'd met through an agency. It was illogical, or at best hypocritical, and she knew it, but she'd found it impossible not to regard this man as pathetic because he'd had recourse to an agency in order to meet someone like her. That she'd been equally willing to subject herself to that humiliation in order to meet someone like him was irrelevant. She knew *she* had a low sense of self-worth, and with age it was increasing. But she didn't want a man like that as well.

Or not that particular man at least.

She and Terry agreed to meet again.

A week later they kissed, and the kiss was prolonged, which led to them going to bed together for the first time in six years. It would have been hard for either to decide whether the experience was more one of familiarity or of estrangement. But the knowledge that both had had other relationships since the last time added something bitter and something sweet to the brief act they performed together, as if it was simultaneously an act of self-vindication and revenge.

Six months later, without telling anyone, they remarried.

THE END

Cf

2008

Colophon Fiction